Man to Man

*Recovering the best of
the male tradition*

A Resource by
Ralph Milton
Illustrated by Don McNair

Editing: Jlm Taylor, Michael Schwartzentruber
Layout and design: Jim Taylor, Michael Schwartzentruber
Illustrations: Don McNair
Cover design: Lois Huey-Heck

Canadian Cataloguing in Publication Data

Milton, Ralph
     Man to Man

ISBN 0-929032-81-0

1. Men—Psychology. 2. Masculinity (Psychology).
I. Title.

HQ1090.M54 1993   305.31   C93-091849-5

Published by
Wood Lake Books Inc.
Box 700, Winfield, BC
Canada V0H 2C0

Printed in Canada by
Hignell Prining Ltd.,
Winnipeg, MB R3G 2B4

To my fathers

Henry Martin Friesen
and
Norman Harry Ingledew

who gave me so much,
and whom I wish I had known better.

Table of Contents

A slice of pumpernickel

Man to Man

A book for men

This is a book for men.

This is not a book for people in the "men's movement." This is for ordinary guys with a home and a mortgage and kids and a job. Guys who vote in elections and try to live decent lives and who don't understand why everybody is on their case all the time.

Maybe you've read in the papers about the "men's lib" types who meet in groups to "let it all hang out" (whatever that means) or who dance naked in the woods. Most of that is media hype. I've been at a few "men's" events, and learned a lot from them. There are always a few on the loony fringe of any movement, and they get their pictures in the paper. Most of us men are simply trying to make sense out of the world we find ourselves in, and sometimes we get together to talk about it.

Hey! Who changed the rules?

Many of us guys woke up one morning to discover that somebody had changed the rules. More than that, somebody had changed the whole ball game. We're standing around wondering what to do next.

We're getting ready for the year 2,000 and wondering what males are going to be like in the third millennium. What is a "real man" anyway? Most men I know are confused and afraid and wondering what the women in our lives expect us to be. Or do. "Will somebody please tell me what the hell is going on here?" is what we're saying.

It's like driving a car in a country where the traffic laws are all different, but nobody will tell you what they are and you can't read the signs. Suddenly a policeman pulls you over and writes you a ticket and you have no idea what you've done wrong.

Women have been very helpful in letting us know what parts of our masculinity don't work anymore. (Let's face it, sometimes they've been brutal. Maybe it was necessary, but it hurt.) Women have **not** been very helpful when it comes to figuring out how we can be real men in a way that works for the year 2,000.

Women don't want us to be women, that much I know. Sure, there may be a few strident feminists who would like to eliminate males altogether, but they are a fringe group. Most of my women friends are feminists (that includes Bev and my daughters Kari and Grace) and they want me to be a man. Male. They have some very definite ideas about what that does **not** mean.

Being a real man does not mean macho. It does not mean superior. It does not mean violent. It does not mean arrogant. It does not mean aggressive. It does not mean rude. It does not mean tough. It does not mean workaholic.

Back in the "good old days" we knew that real men didn't cry. Real men didn't show emotion. Real men never let their fear or confusion show.

In the "good old days" they told us all the things men did not do and they're still telling us what not to do and be and feel. So enough of telling me what a male is not. Will somebody please tell me in words I can understand, what I should be besides nothing?

What are we left with? Should we be a bunch of sad-eyed wimps who mutter, "Yes ma'am," and who ask only, "How high, ma'am?" when women tell us to jump?

No! Women don't want us to be **less** than what we are. Women want us to be **more** than we have been.

But what does that mean?

We can't expect women to answer that question. Women don't know what it's like to be a man any more than men know what it's like to be a woman. Besides, women have their hands full figuring out who **they** are becoming themselves. We guys are going to have to stand on our own hind legs and work out our own masculinity for ourselves.

The good news is that there's lots in the male tradition that is good and helpful. We don't need to throw out everything we have been and all that we thought was important. My father was a good man. There's lots about him that I can appreciate and use. It's there, mixed up with a lot of attitudes that don't work anymore, if they ever did.

The bad news is that sorting the gold from the garbage is no easy thing. If I strip away the crap from the macho myths that we grew up with, there are quality masculine values underneath. We don't have to re-invent masculinity, we simply need to rediscover the genuine article underneath the macho crud. The images, the ideals are all there for us. If we dig down to our roots, we'll find the "right stuff," and then we'll be able to stand up tall, look our sisters in the eye, and celebrate our differences and our common humanity.

The well-known writer C.S. Lewis uses this analogy. When your dog gets its leash wrapped around the fire hydrant, it won't get any-where tugging harder and harder. If the dog keeps going in the same

direction, it only gets tied up tighter and tighter. To move ahead at all, the dog has to back up—to go in the opposite direction for a few feet, to get around the fire hydrant. Sometimes, it has to be dragged in that opposite direction against all its natural instincts.

I'm like that dog. I've growled and snarled and resisted. I feel I've been pushed to go in directions and think about things I'd far sooner avoid. But having been through it, even this old dog realizes it was the right move. Now I can move ahead on life's journey, whereas before I was tied to that hydrant. I'm convinced God was leading me into those somewhat painful changes in direction.

The tapes in our heads

Part of the trouble is that most of us don't know how we managed to get on the wrong side of the hydrant. We have a whole library of little tapes playing in our heads, tapes which keep telling us what it means to be "A Man."

My dad often gave me half-hour talks (yes, I timed them) about morality or ethics or whatever was bugging him at the time. One of his favorite themes was manhood—what it meant to be a "real man." His little sermon (I think he was a frustrated preacher) usually ended with a quote from Rudyard Kipling's poem *If*.

> *If you can keep your head when all about you*
> *Are losing theirs and blaming it on you...*

The poem ended with this ringing call, which dad would recite with
great but controlled emotion, because real men never let their feelings
become too obvious:

> *If you can fill the unforgiving minute*
> *With sixty seconds worth of distance run,*
> *Yours is the Earth, and everything that's in it,*
> *And—which is more—you'll be a Man, my son!*

It's not surprising that I grew up with a tape playing loudly in my
head about things I had to worry over if I wanted to be "A Real Man."
Every one of us has some of those tapes, somewhere.

Stories

Dad also told me stories. There were stories about his growing up
years, about farm life near Rush Lake, Saskatchewan, about our
Mennonite forebears helping each other migrate from Russia to Canada,
about the depression years and our family's struggle to survive. I
learned a lot about who I am from those stories.

The stories I remember best were the ones he made up about Pete
and Nete, two imaginary boys whose mother made them magic cookies.
The brown cookies made them grow bigger, the white ones made them
grow smaller. (When I came across that idea years later in *Alice in
Wonderland,* I thought Lewis Carroll had stolen the idea from my dad.)

Dad imagined all sorts of adventures, often with the active partici-
pation of my sisters and me in the storytelling, adventures of brave
exploits and kindly deeds and wondrous rescues of people in distress.
The stories were never violent. Pete and Nete never used force or hurt
anyone or cheated or lied. Pete and Nete had what Dad called "moral
fibre." They did the right thing, even when it cost.

There is no doubt that Dad used the stories as a teaching vehicle,
and there is no doubt he succeeded to a large degree. I have the Pete-
and-Nete moral-values tape playing loudly in my head too, and with a
bit of editing, they are good and useful values.

There are other tapes in my head—tapes recorded when playing
with my friends, going to school, or while consuming the hundreds of
adventure stories we got from a mail-order library, or from comic
books.

All those tapes, recorded as a young child, play in the background of my mind, subtly informing everything I do. And those tapes keep telling me what it means to be "A Man."

Changing roles

My tapes tell me a real man never loses his cool. He is always in charge of his emotions. A real man can take it (whatever "it" is). A real man knows what is going on. He is always tough and decisive. He is honest, but he is nobody's fool. A real man works hard at a steady job (after "sowing a few wild oats" during his late teens and early twenties), has a wife and kids, and does his duty. A real man can hold his drink. A real man takes charge, especially of his wife and family. A real man is physically stronger than a woman, and can always lift the box or open the jar lid or do any other physically demanding task.

You can add or subtract from that list to suit yourself.

When Bev and I got married more than three decades ago, our roles were clear. She had her tapes playing in her head about being a woman and I had mine about being a man. They were nicely complementary. My job was to conquer the world; hers was to populate it. My job was to "bring home the bacon;" hers was to "bring home the babies."

That tidy little arrangement fell apart when Bev discovered she was a person in her own right, and quite as capable as the man she had married. She challenged her tape and mine, with the result that our marriage hit some pretty rocky places. It almost came apart a couple of times.

Most people congratulate us for staying married to each other for so many years. But we've only stayed married in a very literal sense. Both of us have changed. A lot. I couldn't have stayed married to the naive girl who walked down the aisle way back then. And I don't think she'd put up today with the arrogant jock who borrowed money from her to buy a suit to get married in.

We are very different people now. In that sense, I'm not married to the same woman, and she isn't married to the same man.

Blame everything on the army

I love to blame the feminist movement on the generals who got us into World War II. A friend, who has spent his life in the military, gets absolutely livid when I blame the army for the feminist movement, and we have a fine argument. If he didn't see some truth in my statement, he wouldn't get so upset.

During World War II, almost every able-bodied man went off to Europe to fight and the women took over their jobs. My mother found herself working in an office in Ottawa and for the first time in her life, having a paycheque made out in her name. The song they played on the radio was *Rosie the Riveter*, who discovered she could do "man's work." And when Johnnie came marching home, he found that Rosie wasn't about to give up her job or her new-found independence and her paycheque. Women discovered that, except for muscle bulk, they had everything they needed to compete in the job market.

I also argue that the Pentagon got the "men's movement" started during the Vietnam War. It became obvious that many men broke down under the pressures of war. We pinned hero medals on emotional shells who came back from the war with their personalities destroyed. Some of those men began to ask the kinds of questions we're talking about in this book.

Sure, the men's movement and the feminist movement have lots of other roots—like the automobile, education, and Florence Nightingale. More recently, the birth-control pill and the computer have been major factors.

The computer? You bet. One of the bigwigs from the Microsoft Corporation was quoted recently in our local paper as saying, "In the year 2,000, everything from the neck down will be minimum wage." In other words, the muscles and size which always gave us a physical advantage over women are now important only in professional sports.

Painful process

All this change has been really painful for us guys. Over and over, those little tapes tell us to act one way, while the women we love and the society we live in tell us something very different.

It seems we have two options for dealing with our dilemma.

We can get mad. We can refuse to change. A lot of men are taking that route nowadays. A good many of them end up so mad they take their anger out on somebody. Too often, they do it on their wives and children. They beat up the people closest to them. If you are one of those men, you'd better put this book down right now and go see your doctor or a professional counselor, quick!

The second option is to get some perspective on ourselves and on what's bugging us. The best way I know to get that kind of perspective is to learn to laugh a bit. I don't mean to laugh it off, to pretend our troubles don't exist, to say they don't matter. But if I can see the humor in my situation, I can let that humor untangle my jangled nerves.

If I can laugh, I'm far more likely to be realistic about my problems.

Healing humor

I have a close friend who is dying of a form of cancer. I sent him a whole box full of my joke books so he can work on his personal "humor therapy." He's a medical doctor, so he knows the jokes are certainly no substitute for medical treatment. "But," he says, "humor helps me heal my spirit."

> *God will yet fill your mouth*
> *with laughter,*
> *And your lips*
> *with shouts of joy.*
> Job 8:21

A friend asked me recently to help unload his furniture. "We're looking for guys with strong backs and weak minds," he grinned.

"Would you settle for a guy with a weak back **and** a weak mind?" I asked. I'm well past 50-something and not everything (the big exception is my appetite) works as well as it used to. There are only two remedies. Exercise and laughter.

But humor's a tricky thing. Like so many of God's gifts, it cuts two ways. It can heal and it can hurt.

Have you heard this joke, for example?

> *Why do all the space missions have a female astronaut on board?*
> *So someone will ask for directions if they get lost out there.*

If that gag has a familiar feel to it, it should. It's a recycled version of one of those "dumb blonde" jokes that went around not so long ago. Here's a bunch more:

> *What's a man's idea of helping out with the housework?*
> *Lifting his legs so you can vacuum.*

> *What's the difference between a man and ET?*
> *ET had sense enough to phone home.*

> *Why is psychoanalysis quicker for men than for women?*
> *When it's time to go back to his childhood, he's already there.*

How do men do exercises at the beach?
By sucking in their bellies every time they see a bikini.

What does a man consider to be a seven-course meal?
A hot dog and a six-pack.

Make you squirm a bit, don't they? I got them from John Hole, an engineer, who had photocopied a batch of them and was handing them out before church one morning. I showed my copy to Patricia Baker, one of our ministers. She laughed and immediately headed for the photocopier. She made three copies.

What's funny? What's not?

I (and I suspect the other guys at the church) laughed just a bit louder than necessary at those jokes. Because hidden down inside every joke is a kernel of painful truth. That's what makes them funny.

If it doesn't contain that kernel of truth, if it perpetuates injustice, if someone finds it offensive, a joke isn't funny. Period.

One of Canada's federal cabinet ministers joked about sexual harassment in an after-dinner speech. "I've never been the object of sexual harassment," he said, "but if I had been so honored, I'd want to have it known."

A flip comment about sexual harassment doesn't quite find me in stitches because I have a daughter who had to put up with the wandering hands of her boss when she was waiting on tables in Vancouver. That, or lose her job. She finally quit even though she had no job to go to, then was criticized by the unemployment insurance people for having quit her job "for no good reason."

A provincial politician got into hot water recently by telling this old clunker.

The guy picks up his mail-order bride at the train station. He puts her on the buggy and says "Giddap" to the horse. The horse doesn't move. Whack! The man hits the horse with a whip. "That's one!" he says.

Still the horse doesn't move. Whack! goes the whip again, a bit more viciously "That's two," says the man.

The horse still doesn't move. Whack goes the whip. This time he really lays it into the horse's back. Nothing happens. "That's three!" says the man. And he hauls out a pistol and shoots the horse.

His new bride gave him hell. "Why did you shoot that poor horse?"

she berated him. "That was a terrible thing to do."
The man waited quietly until she had finished. "That's one!" he said.

It was just a joke!

These politicians didn't know what hit them when a whole variety
of women dropped great brown loads on them from the stratosphere of
their indignation. "Sexist pig!" was among the kinder things the women
said. The guys thought they were telling a joke, just to get a laugh. "I
didn't mean anything by it!" they claimed.

The politicians' problem is not so much that they told those jokes.
Their problem was that they really had no idea what the fuss was about.
They were insensitive to the genuine pain that victims—especially
women—feel.

But is there anything essentially different between the "dumb men"
jokes I got from John Hole and the jokes of the two politicians?

Yes. But maybe no.

The politicians' jokes make light of violence. The reality is that, in
far too many instances, women are no more highly regarded and treated
no better than a horse. Hundreds of women have been murdered as
casually as that horse was shot.

Knowing that takes the giggle out of the joke for me, especially
when a very close friend was treated like that horse during years of a
terrible marriage. She was beaten regularly, and often spent the entire
night having locked herself in the furnace room, just so she wouldn't be
beaten any more.

So when I hear those politicians, I think of very specific people

---

Then the question: Where does laughter come from? It comes from as
deep a place as tears come from, and in a way it comes from the same
place. As much as tears do, it comes out of the darkness of the world
where God is of all missing persons the most missed, except that it
comes not as an ally of darkness but as its adversary, not as a symptom
of darkness but as its antidote.

Frederick Buechner,
*Telling the Truth: the Gospel as Tragedy, Comedy
& Fairy Tale,*
Harper & Row, Publishers, 1977

who have been victims, and I get mad as hell.

Jokes are not funny when they have a victim. When somebody feels put down, or has their pain trivialized, humor becomes violence.

Except when people are in positions of power. Then I think it's fair ball to use humor to bring them down a couple of notches. And in our society, men are generally in a position of power over women. To that extent, my dumb male jokes are OK. To the extent that they hurt men who already feel powerless, they are not OK.

Separating the wheat from the chaff

So how do we know what's good and what's bad, the healing from the hurting? Well, we don't always. But we have to keep trying anyway.

It helps if we tell each other what we believe.

You see, I think most men are essentially good. Genuinely good. But we often don't act on that essential goodness because we've never stopped to look at ourselves long enough to figure out who we really are. We play-act instead of being our true, genuine selves.

So I'll start by trying to tell you what I believe. Or at least some of it:

1. **There's nobody quite like me.** That sounds conceited, but it's true of everybody. Every flower is different. Every snowflake is different. And God created each man and each woman as a unique human being. We men should no more attempt to be copies of women than we should be copies of each other.
2. **God loves me.** Me, specifically—personally—in the same way that God cares for you specifically and personally. God doesn't care more for women than for men—or vice versa. God doesn't have favorites, be it race, nation, sex, or profession.
3. **God wants me to like you.** And everyone else I meet. If I can sometimes crank that up a notch or two and turn "like" into "love," God is delighted. That's why, if my thoughts or my actions hurt you, or anyone else, God hurts. God hurts, and would really like it if I make the necessary changes so that I'm no longer hurting you. Or anyone else.
4. **God lets me be in charge of me.** God wants me to make those changes, but God doesn't force me. And because God also lets you be in charge of you, I can't make you change. The only person I can change is me. And the only person you can change is you.
5. **God would love to give me a hand, but I have to ask.** And I have a

strong hunch you'd be willing to give me a hand too, if I asked. In fact, it just may be that God would act through you to give me a hand with my attitudes and actions. If I ask. And the reverse would also be true. So it's really important that you and I talk eyeball to eyeball, because God is just itching to act through each of us to help the other. We're not alone.

Given that "creed," you and I can use those "dumb men" jokes to face up to who we are and how we respond to other people. We can begin being honest with each other by laughing together at those jokes in each other's company, and perhaps not using them with men we don't know too well. (Not all jokes are suitable for all situations.) And when we've finished laughing, and maybe crying a little, we can say, "OK. That's stuff I have to work on. Can I get a bit of help from you and God?"

When Patricia hands those jokes to her women friends, I hope their laughter will help them not lose hope for the men in the their lives, or for themselves as they wrestle with the dark side of their own personalities. Humor is a wonderful antidote to despair, especially when we can laugh with each other, rather than at each other.

The best humor gets close to the bone and is funny precisely because there's truth in it. It always walks right on the edge of being painful. When John Hole hands those jokes out to his friends, he's handing out mirrors in which we may get a helpful glimpse of ourselves. If we look in those mirrors and see there a person made in the "image of God" (check out Genesis 1:27 in the Bible), a person who is laughing at least a little, then we've got a pretty good chance of making something good out of our lives.

But look out! Have you noticed that most comedians are men? There are delightful exceptions (Lily Tomlin is one of my favorites) but for the most part, the comics are male. Maybe women don't need humor in the same way men do. Generally, women have superior social skills. Most women know how to talk to each other. Men are more likely to compete with each other. When men get together, they tell jokes and engage in verbal horseplay, because that is kind of a mock competition. We use humor to avoid talking with any seriousness about the things that trouble us most. We hide behind our jokes, to avoid facing the things that really matter to us.

Runaway humor

Jack Lemmon made a fine movie out of a stage play called "A Thousand Clowns." It was about a guy everybody liked because he was full of fun and always had a joke to tell and was just generally the life of the party. Then he discovered he had only a few months to live, and wanted to renew a relationship with his estranged wife and his adult son. But his own humor tripped him up. His wife and son were sick and tired of him making a joke out of everything, never taking them seriously. So they walked out.

That hit me where I live. I saw big Ralph in the character Lemmon played. I can be the life of the party when I'm in the mood. And it is fun kibitzing with my kids and with Bev. But too often, when family talk is about things of deep importance, a smart remark or flip comment occurs to me. If I let it out, it can be devastating.

The biblical parallel

King David is one of my favorite biblical characters. Like me, David could foul up royally. He was a high diver who plunged in at the deep end, and sometimes whacked his head on the shallow bottom.

I see so much of myself in David—just as I did in some of those "dumb men" jokes—that I decided to do some serious study of the guy. Up to that point, about all I knew about David was that he killed Goliath and had a steamy affair with Bathsheba.

Biblical soap opera

I had always thought of King David as a paragon of virtue. The best king Israel ever had. A model of manhood. Early Christian writers made a particular point of showing how Jesus was descended from King David, Israel's greatest King.

I'd heard bits and pieces of the story in church, but when I sat down and read the whole thing through, just like a novel, I was rocked right down to my socks. The story of David reads like a TV soap opera—like Dallas, which you can still see in re-runs. It had all the sex and violence and cheating and foulness of anything on TV.

But it had something that Dallas didn't have—a sense of nobility. The biblical characters are not one-dimensional like most of the folks on TV. They are complex, full of all the stuff that make us humans so interesting. Full of all the kindness and the cruelty that make us so wonderfully and tragically human. And they had a genuine sense that

God was somehow involved in
their lives—not something
you'd notice in the characters
on Dallas.

David's story is a great
example of why the Bible
makes such a good source book
for learning about the life we
have to live here in the last bit
of this century. Unlike many
religious writings, the Hebrew
scriptures show us the good
and the bad and the in-between of its many characters. We have good
examples and bad examples, and David was both.

If we imagine ourselves into David's story, we'll understand more
of ourselves.

And what a story! David was anything but a plaster saint on a pedestal.
He was tough, passionate, ruthless, caring, horny, short-tempered, forgiving. And like most men, he had a terrible time being a father. No, he didn't
have trouble conceiving children. He had trouble being a father.

David did some things most of us would be pretty ashamed of.
When David raped Bathsheba and got her pregnant, he used every trick
in the book to avoid facing up to what he'd done. Among other things,
he got Bathsheba's husband totally tanked one night, thinking he would
go back, sleep with his wife, and think the kid was his. When that didn't
work, David had the man killed.

(David cared too, very deeply, though he tried not to let it show.
The bright side to the story of his rape of Bathsheba is that David really
learned to love her and the child of his adultery. When the child died,
David knew how much he had loved that baby.)

David was a killer, all right. In one section of his story in the Bible,
the text goes on and on about one battle after another where David and
his gang massacred one city after another. Sickening and boring.

There was no Geneva Convention at that time. Losers had no rights.
No prisoners were taken, except those you wanted to keep as slaves—
usually the women and children. David and his army would go out,
challenge the army of one of the small cities within marching distance. The
folks in those cities had two choices. Surrender and pay huge amounts of
money and food to David for the privilege of staying alive. Or fight. And if

they lost, everybody was killed, everything of value was taken by the army (that was the soldier's "pay"), and the city was burned.

Some of David's killing was more personal. He arranged to have various enemies dispatched. Political infighting was not very subtle in those days.

In many ways, David was just like every other successful king or emperor of his time. "Love your enemies" wasn't even given lip service. The rule was, "Do unto others before they do unto you."

We can hardly even imagine the violence of the time in which King David lived. At one point, I was tempted to throw the Bible in the corner and say, "Who needs this? God doesn't order people to commit genocide!" But I kept on reading, and I think I came to a more useful understanding of David's story.

David played the power game. He played it hard, and he played it ruthlessly—the way it is still played in corporate boardrooms around the world—pitting one man against another, eliminating any that he considered a threat to his own power. In our day, people are not generally killed in those power struggles, but they are often destroyed. Our contemporary power struggles are just as ruthless, though maybe not quite as bloody.

And when David went to war, he waged war in the same way and according to the same standards that everyone in his day accepted.

"Well, you've totally destroyed King David for me," said a man at the Banff Men's Conference, the first time I led a workshop on David. "I always thought he was a noble person. Now you've turned him into a third-rate thug. A killer."

Don't get me wrong. I'm not setting out to ruin the Bible for you or to destroy King David's reputation. It's just that David and the other folks in the Bible were very real people. And the genius of the Bible is that it tells it like it was, without hiding any of the seamy side of the people involved. Many of the stories in the Bible are exactly the kind of stories men love (and women often hate), which may be why they are in the Bible.

A typical example is the story of the Philistine foreskins. Has your minister ever talked about the Philistine foreskins from the pulpit? Probably not. I've never heard the story read in church, but it's there in the Bible (1 Samuel 18:20-29) along with a few other incidents you'll never hear about unless you read the Bible for yourself.

It's a story about one of those grand, dramatic gestures that David loved. During the hostilities between King Saul and David, before David himself became king, Saul challenged David to circumcise 100 of the Philistine enemy. David did it, and proved it by presenting his trophies to Saul.

When I told that story to the group of guys at the Banff Men's Conference, some of them squirmed and crossed their legs and covered the family jewels. I don't blame them. If I hadn't been the big performer telling the story, I'd have been protecting my privates too.

Besides, it's just too easy to label David a "third-rate thug" and leave it at that. To look back from our "enlightened" 20th century perspective and call David a murderer is arrogant. David lived by the light he had, and in the light of his day, it was smart and noble to kill your enemies. According to the morality of his time, the only morality he knew, David was, for the most part, a good man. Clearly the biblical writers, who shared his moral system, thought he was pretty wonderful.

I don't think it's fair to judge people of another time by today's morality. It gives us a nice feeling of superiority. We feel noble by comparison. But we don't learn anything from feelings of superiority—either about them, or about ourselves.

Getting carried away

Once I got my head around that hurdle, I could read the story of David and discover that he really was a unique person. Yes, he was a killer. But he was also a kind, caring man who struggled hard to hear what God wanted; a brilliant leader who fought for and brought unparalleled prosperity to his people; a passionate, charismatic religious leader who sometimes got a little carried away.

Did he get carried away! There's the time David was bringing the ark into Jerusalem. The ark was the most important religious symbol in his country, and bringing it to Jerusalem was an important part of David's dream for his nation. He pulled out all the stops for the celebration of the century, and got so carried away that he danced down the road wearing nothing much except an ephod, a kind of an apron. That display of the royal hangings had the whole town talking and got Michal, one of his wives, flaming mad.

There are other stories that show us David's passion. When his best friend Jonathan was killed in battle, David sang a song of mourning that is achingly beautiful—a song that still moves our hearts today. And when David cried over Absalom, his son, we can hear the cry of every father who has lost a son, especially a son estranged from his father.

Learning to love

David fathered a lot of kids, but he had a hard time being much of a father. So his relationship with his children was not wonderful, and the last part of the story is mostly about his boys trying to take the old man's throne away from him. It really wasn't until David was quite old that he began to understand what it means to be a father. In the end, he does manage a father-son relationship with Solomon.

And David learns how to love a woman. He'd had sex with all his wives and dozens of concubines, but had never had anything close to a real relationship. His famous rape of Bathsheba led him to commit an ugly, cowardly murder—a sordid affair in which Bathsheba was nothing but a victim. But Bathsheba was a strong, intelligent person and in the end, David learned to respect and to love her.

A role model

Within the person of David I can see the kind of man who builds empires while destroying people, then destroys himself because what he really wanted most of all was the love and affection of the people he destroyed. As I said earlier, I think most men are good, but we don't always know how to **be** good. So in David I see a reflection of myself and of many of the men I know who learn to love too late in their lives.

I look back on the story of David, and I can learn from his bright side as well as from his dark side. I can see in David an extreme, almost caricatured, expression of the feelings and attitudes I see in myself. I may not express myself as physically as David, and I certainly don't have a kingdom or an army through which to act out my lust for power. But I do express it. David was a man of his time and I am a man of my time, and our attitudes and perspectives are not that different. David's are simply shown to us in brilliant story and color, and that's what makes his story so useful.

Tell a story

My favorite way of getting inside a story and learning from it, is to retell the story in my own words. There's nothing new about that. The Hebrews who gave us our Old Testament, and Jesus who was raised in that tradition, knew how to do that. It's the tradition of the Aggadah. In order to understand a story, you tell another story. And another. And another, until the light dawns.

My purpose in writing this book is not to tell you what is right or wrong or how you should think and feel. My purpose is to let you see inside **David's story** and inside **my story** so that you can see inside **your own story** too.

So each of the five chapters that follow have the same format. I suggest that you first read David's story from the Bible. Then I retell part of that story in my own words, I tell some of my story, and then I let fly with sort of a sermon. I guess I inherited my Dad's tendency to preach. All of that, I hope, will loosen up some of your story in your head.

Using this book

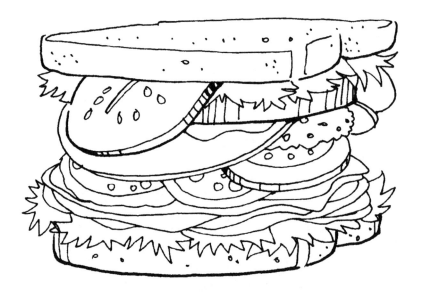

This book is not just for reading. It's for working with. Either by yourself, or in a group. If you simply read it straight through, like a novel, you'll probably come out confused at best, and more likely upset. You have to put something of yourself into this process too.

The book as a whole is constructed like a Dagwood sandwich. The opening chapter—the one you just read—and the closing chapter are like the slices of pumpernickel bread on the top and bottom of the sandwich.

In between—the middle five chapters—is the filling. And each of these five chapters follows the same pattern. You can think of them as the slice of kosher dill pickle (David's story), a slice of baloney (a bit of my story), and a dash of hot mustard (a reflection on our common story). The real meat in the sandwich you add yourself, as you tie in your story.

Just to make it easier, I've broken each of the middle five chapters, the filling in the sandwich, down into those four parts:

David's story—the kosher dill pickle. This is my retelling of the story from the Bible. In each case, I tell you where you can find the original story in the Bible. I tell the story in my own words from my perspective, hoping you'll check it out in the Bible yourself to find out how many liberties I've taken. And I admit to taking quite a few.

My story—the slice of baloney. David's story almost always shakes loose some of my own story. So I tell you an incident from my life that connects with something in the David story. And I hope that from time to time, you'll say, "Milton, that really is baloney!"

Our story—a dash of hot mustard. One of my less flattering friends calls this "The Long Boring Sermon." This is my reflection on the stories you've just read. I try and put into words what I think it means. I hope you don't agree with everything I say here, either.

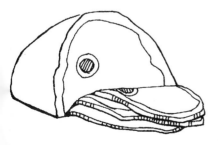

Your story—the real meat in the sandwich. This part isn't in the book, of course. But I give you some questions that I hope will prompt you to tell some of your story. To yourself, if necessary. But it's better if you can share your story with some friends, perhaps in a formal group organized for that purpose, perhaps just at the coffee counter somewhere. I hope you'll take this opportunity to talk about an incident in your own life, or to write it down, or at least to think about it.

All this stuff only means something when it connects with your own life. Otherwise it's a sandwich full of empty calories.

Reading the Bible

Here's a couple of suggestions that'll make it easier to read the story of David in the Bible.

At the top of each of the five middle chapters, you'll find listed the biblical passages that I used in my retelling. If you take a highlighting marker, you could highlight those portions in your Bible. Or simply put a line down the side of the column of the text that we've used. That'll make it easier to read the story all the way through without having to stop to look up which verses to read.

I suggest you start by reading the whole David story through in one sitting (it won't take you that long). That way you'll get a sense of the sweep of this saga. Then you can decide whether you want to re-read the specific portions before you read my re-tellings of them. If I succeed and get you really hooked on the story, maybe you'll want to read the parts I left out. Who knows, I may have missed the most important part of the story!

A personal request—please don't use that dusty old *King James Version* of the Bible your mother gave you. The old English is beautiful but too hard to understand. It uses Shakespearean English, which is beautiful but terribly dated. You almost have to read the *King James Version* in mournful tones wearing your best Sunday suit. And you'll think of it as Holy Writ. I'd prefer you to think of it as a rollicking good story that connects with your story in a whole lot of ways.

My favorite translation is the *New Revised Standard Version*. It's the newest and I think the best of the translations. But the *Good News* translation (officially called *Today's English Version*) is also good, as is the *New Jerusalem Bible* and the *New International Version*. If you don't own one of the newer translations, it's high time you did.

I hope you'll discover, as I did, that each re-telling of the biblical saga gets you understanding a bit more of what was in the original biblical text. I'm not saying I now understand what the story in the Bible "means." In fact, I don't think there is a "meaning" to the original story at all, other than to show how rich and powerful the Hebrews

were in King David's day. But the story does speak to me. It helps me
to understand myself, to see who I am and where God is calling me.
The story will probably say different things to you. God doesn't always
tell each of us the same thing any more than a parent says exactly the
same thing to each child.

Don't forget to laugh

Most of all, don't take anything too seriously.

Don't take my retelling of the biblical stories too seriously—they're
intended only to get you to look at the real thing in a new light.

Don't take the stories in the Bible itself too seriously either—
remember that they were flesh-and-blood people, with all of the foibles
and failings that we have, and then some. Some of the stories in the
Bible are in there because the guys just enjoyed telling good stories. We
still do. And if we could read the story in the original language, we'd
see there's a fair bit of humor in it as well.

And above all, don't take yourself too seriously. Your stories, good
or bad, are not etched in stone, like grave markers. They are stepping
stones, to allow you to learn from life and to move on. Well, they're not
all stones. Some are banana peels and you may slip and fall on your
backside. That's OK. We'll help you up.

Humor is one of God's great gifts. If you read this stuff and have a
bit of a chuckle at King David, at me, and at yourself, you'll grow. At
least a little. If you talk about it with your friends, all of you may find a
little direction.

Which brings us back to the "dumb male" jokes.

Why did Moses spend 40 years in the wilderness?
Because even then men refused to ask for directions.

It's a brand new wilderness we're wandering around in, guys. The
directions toward authentic manhood are there, but many of them are
smudgy and hard to read. Sometimes it feels as if we are lost in outer
space. More often it's the inner space, the confusions in our heads and
bellies that keep us from finding the real men God calls us to be.

It's time to swallow hard and ask for directions. What better place
to look for directions than in the Bible, and in our own experience as
men?

The good stuff

Chapter 1

Men compete

David's story

Part I
from shepherd to hero to fugitive

*A loose paraphrase of selected portions from
1 Samuel.*
Chapter 17:1–18:16
Chapter 18:20–20:3
Chapter 20:30–20:42

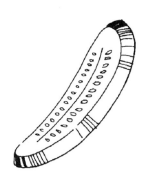

So.

The Philistines and the Israelites were having a war. Saul was king
of the Israelites. The Philistines were all lined up on one side of the
valley, the Israelites on the other. The whole thing looked an awful lot
like the start of the Super Bowl.

All this happened about a thousand years before the time of Jesus.
The story in the Bible is told from the Israelite point of view, so naturally they are the good guys and the Philistines are the bad guys.

The Philistines had a superstar named Goliath, about twice the size
of your average fullback. He was nine and a half feet tall—all decked
out in a brass hat and iron jock strap.

Goliath bellowed across the valley. "Hey, you guys are cowards.
Wimps. Pick out your toughest guy and we'll go at it one on one.
Winner take all."

The story isn't about Goliath, though. It's about a teenager named
David who lived on a farm back in Bethlehem, working for Jesse, his
dad. David was the youngest of eight brothers. The three oldest brothers
were off in that battle with Saul, glaring at the Philistines across the
valley and worrying about Goliath.

So Jesse said to David. "Those brothers of yours must be starved.

Here's some bread and some corn. Take it to them. Oh, and take these ten cheeses to the Major in charge of their division. It won't hurt to keep the old man happy. Then hurry back and let me know how they're doing."

So David got up at the crack of dawn and headed off with his bread and corn and cheese and found his brothers and delivered everything as per instructions. And of course, he stayed to take in a bit of the fight. David saw the uptight Israelites glaring across the valley at the Philistines and their giant, Goliath. And sure enough big Goliath came up and yelled the same thing all over again. "Pick out your toughest guy and we'll go at it one on one. Winner take all."

"Are you just going to stand here and let that jerk make us look like a bunch of nerds?" David demanded. "We've got Yahweh our God on our side, right?"

"Look, twerp!" said David's older brother. "Who's lookin' after those sheep of yours? Go wrestle one of them ewes. They're more your speed. Don't come up here and tell us how to fight our war."

"Hey, don't get your shirt in a knot!" said David. "I was just asking."

David walked away from his brothers, but he kept going among the rest of the troops asking the same kind of question. Eventually, word got to Saul, and Saul said, "Let me talk to the kid."

"I'll knock this guy off. No problem." David stood there looking like the typical cocky teenager.

"You're just a kid," said Saul. "This Goliath is twice your size and he's been fighting all his life. You haven't got a snowball's chance in hell."

"Oh yeah?" said David. "Sure, I don't know much about fighting giants. But looking after sheep is no wimpish job, y'know. I've knocked off lions and wolves and bears. I can knock off this Rambo the same way. Besides, I've got Yahweh on my side."

"What do you mean, Yahweh's on your side?"

"Yahweh. Our God, remember? Yahweh helped me kill the lions and the bears. Yahweh will help me with that big jerk."

Saul swallowed hard. "You realize we're playing 'winner take all?' Nobody else has the guts to go up against that man. If you blow it, we're all done for."

David didn't back down at all.

"At least take my equipment. Here's my brass hat and my chain-link jacket," Saul said.

David put on Saul's armor and tried to walk. "I can't wear this stuff. I can hardly move."

"Whatever you say," said Saul. "I just hope you know what you're doing."

David found five smooth stones in a creek nearby and put them in his fanny pack. And he took his sling. That's all. Down into the bottom of the valley he went to meet Goliath. There wasn't a man in that whole Israelite army who expected David to come back alive. Or themselves,

either, if he lost.

Goliath almost had a bird when he saw young David coming up to him. "You little sawed-off runt. I'll make mincemeat out of you."

"Hey, Goliath," said David. "You've got a sword and all that armor and you're nine feet tall, but listen, I've got God on my side."

"Ha!" yelled the giant.

So David reached in his fanny pack, took one of the stones, and put it in the pouch of his sling. He whirled it round his head and let fly.

Whack! Everybody in the valley could hear the stone hit Goliath's forehead. David ran over, took Goliath's own sword, and chopped off the giant's head. With that, the whole Philistine army turned tail and ran.

It was a slaughter. The Israelites chased the Philistines, chopping and hacking and pillaging and taking no prisoners.

When David came back from chasing Philistines, Saul asked him, "Who are your folks, son?"

"My dad is Jesse. We live in Bethlehem."

"Well, we're mighty glad you're here, David. You're going to come and live with me in the royal palace, see. I'd like you to meet my son, Jonathan."

Sure enough, the two boys became friends. Best buds. Soul mates. Jonathan kept giving fancy presents to David, like his sword and his bow and his fancy cummerbund.

David did a lot of growing in the next few years. It wasn't long

before he became Saul's right hand man. A five-star general! People
called him a "child prodigy."

One day, when David was coming back from another war (it was
the Philistines again), the whole city came out for a welcome-home
parade. All the women were lining the streets, singing and dancing and
yelling and carrying on like cheerleaders at a football game.

They began singing a little ditty, over and over again.

Saul has whopped a thousand,
But David's whopped ten thousand.

When Saul heard that, he hit the roof. "What in blazes is going on here?
They're saying David is ten times the man I am? What else does he
want? My life? My job?"

That kind of soured the relationship between David and the king.
Besides, Saul had problems of his own. Saul suffered from chronic
depression and migraine headaches and there seemed to be very little he
or anyone could do about it. David played on his harp and sang for the
old man. That helped a little. But lately, even that didn't seem to be
working. "The old guy's losing it," people began to whisper around the
palace.

Sometimes Saul would completely flip out. One day while David
was plunking away on his harp, Saul tried to pin him to the wall with
his spear. David ducked, just in time. Saul tried again, but David moved
the way Wayne Gretsky avoids a bodycheck.

"Get out of my palace," yelled Saul. "And General David, you are
hereby demoted to Major."

Kicking David out of the palace didn't help Saul one bit. It seemed
to Saul as if nothing worked out for him, but everything seemed to
work out for David. David was a good fighter, a good leader, a good
politician. David shrugged off all the compliments. "God helps me," he
simply said.

Saul began to actively hate David, and started to make devious
plans to get rid of him. Then one of the palace gossips told him, "Your
daughter Michal has the hots for David."

"Aha!" thought Saul. "That'll work out just fine." So the king
called in one of his flunkies. "Listen. Go tell David he can marry
Michal, but he's got to earn her first. I want him to go and bring me
back 100 Philistine foreskins."

"Hey!" said David. "I wouldn't mind being the king's son-in-law. What's so hard about finding a few foreskins?"

Men don't generally consent to having their foreskins amputated without a little discussion, and the Philistines were no exception. But David took along a bunch of his army buddies and in no time at all, they had two hundred Philistine foreskins.

David brought that gory collection to King Saul who almost tossed his cookies when he saw it. And David told him all the sordid details of how he and his friends "persuaded" the Philistines. Saul had no choice but to let Michal move in with David.

Needless to say, this didn't make Saul feel better. He lay awake nights trying to think of ways to terminate David. Meanwhile, David was going up in the public opinion polls and Saul was going down.

Saul tried to get help from his son Jonathan. But Jonathan spilled the beans to David, and the two of them tried to figure a way out of the mess.

"I'll talk to Dad," said Jonathan. Which he did. "David hasn't done anything to you, Dad," said Jonathan. "He killed Goliath for you. He's always been on your side. What have you got against him?"

"You're right, you're right," said Saul. "Tell David, it's OK. I won't hurt him."

Things were good for awhile. But then there was another war with the Philistines, and Saul's depression was so bad, he couldn't make it to the front lines. David (who was the General again) went out and of course did everything right, which infuriated Saul.

When David got home, Saul tried to pin him to the wall with the spear again, but David ducked and ran.

This time Saul was a bit more determined, and he sent his guards to David's house with instructions to kill David when he came out in the morning to go to work.

But Michal spotted them. "You've got to run, David," she told him. She made a rope out of a bunch of sheets, and let him down through the

window at the back of the house. Then she made up the bed, complete
with a mop for the head, to make it look as if David was asleep there,
just to give him a bit more of a head start.

Saul was really angry at Michal. "Why, Michal?" he demanded.
"Why did you tell lies to your poor old dad?"

"I had no choice," Michal lied. "David would have killed me if I
hadn't."

David headed off looking for help from his old friend Samuel.
Samuel was a prophet who was holding old-fashioned revival meetings
at a place called Naioth. When Saul found out where David was, he sent
some of his senior staff people after him. But they went to one of
Samuel's revival services, got religion, and freaked out.

So Saul sent another bunch. They got religion too. Saul sent a third
bunch. Same result.

"If you want something done right, you've got to do it yourself,"
Saul grumbled. So he took his migraines and headed out toward Naioth.
But even old Saul got religion. And did he get saved! He stripped off
his clothes and ran around starkers yelling, "Thank you, Moses!"

"I'm outa here," said David, and decided it was time to have a little
conversation with Jonathan.

Jonathan didn't know what to do either. "Dad is really acting pretty
strange, but I don't think he means you any harm, David."

"Tell me about it," said David. "He wants me skinned alive, that's all."

"Yeah. I guess." Jonathan was really down. "I'm caught between a
rock and a hard place, David. You've played by the rules and you're
winning the game. Dad's been a real s.o.b. Theoretically, I should
inherit the kingdom when he goes, but you and I and everybody but him
knows that God wants you to be king."

"If you're worried about what will happen to you, Jonathan, if I got
to be king, well...dammit...we're best friends."

"So it's going to be OK. Somehow. Somewhere. Sometime."

Jonathan tried several times to argue with his father on David's
behalf. It didn't work. Once Saul got so upset, he even threw a spear at
his own son.

"You bastard," yelled Saul. "I know how much you like that son-
of-a-bitch. Well, he's dead meat, you hear? He's dead meat."

Jonathan and David arranged to meet in a field way outside of the
city. "It's no good," said Jonathan. "There's no going back. You've got
to get away from here, fast."

Somehow the two men knew this would be their last meeting. There seemed to be nothing to say, and yet somehow everything needed to be said.

They kissed each other. They cried. Then Jonathan said to David, "Go in peace, David, knowing that we have made promises to each other before God, that God's love will always be between you and me, and between our descendants, forever."

Then David walked off into the wilderness. And Jonathan walked back into the city.

My story

How I became a
successful nerd

When I was nine years old they called me "Slug." It wasn't such a bad name. It just meant I was short and a bit dumpy.

By the time I got through high-school, they called me "Slim." I liked that better than Slug.

It was getting from Slug to Slim that ruined any chances I had of being a "real man." During my early teens I grew like a melon in a manure pile. Four inches in one year. From being the shortest kid in my crowd, I became the tallest.

I was well into my 20s when my head figured out what size my body was and I stopped tripping over the pattern on the linoleum. In the meantime, the damage to my male ego was enormous.

When I went from grade nine to grade ten, I transferred from a small, one-room country school to a large many-roomed city high school in Winnipeg. It was bad enough being the identifiable hayseed from a town nobody had ever heard of. But I had to try out for the various teams. "Mandatory for all males," read the instruction sheet.

So dutifully, I showed up for basketball. The coach was impressed. "Good height." He handed me a basketball. I could put my hand on the top of the ball and lift it right off the floor. My hand was huge.

"Impressive," said the coach. "Let's see you shoot a basket." I missed the backboard. I tried a second and a third time. "I think," said the coach, trying to be diplomatic, "they'd really like to have you on the football team. You'd make a great linebacker."

"Let's see you kick a field goal," said the football coach. I kalumped up to the ball, swung my enormous foot, missed the ball by a country mile and broke three fingers in the hand of the kid who was holding it.

His fingers healed faster than my ego.

"Ahh...have you thought of trying out for the literary society or the glee club?" the football coach smirked.

That's how I became a nerd.

A hayseed with big hands and feet who got his jollies out of songs and sonnets. I couldn't do science and math either for reasons that were far less obvious. Math and science get you lots more macho points than literature or music.

I had serious doubts about my own sexuality until Bev and I were married when it seemed we could conceive kids just by holding hands. What a relief that was. "If I'm not man enough to compete," I thought, "at least I can sire some kids."

I didn't realize back in high school just how much I was competing anyway. I couldn't win at football or math, but I could compete and win lots of mind games. I could out-think and out-talk many other students. I played very competitive games with words. And ideas.

The debating team, for instance. Essay and poetry contests. I even ran for President of the Student Council and won.

Sure, lots more girls hung around the guys who could score in sports. Especially contact sports. But some of the girls hung around with the artsy crowd too. And there was nothing like the presence of a

---

The masculine attitude toward life was, "I feel good today; I'll go out and kill something." Tribes fought for their existence, and so the work of the warrior was held to be the most glorious of all; indeed it was the only work that counted. The woman's part consisted of tilling the soil, gathering the food, tanning the skins and fashioning garments, brewing the herbs, raising the children, dressing the warriors' wounds, looking after the herds, and any other light and airy trifle which might come to her notice.

Nellie McClung
quoted in *No Small Legacy* by Carol Hancock
Wood Lake Books

few females to get us males competing. It may have been coincidence, but my very first "steady" girlfriend happened at the time I won a lead in our school operetta.

The Mikado. I played the title role. The Mikado is the macho part in that silly operetta. Even though he's an utter ass, the Mikado gets to bounce around the stage intimidating people. Not a bad fantasy for a teenager who can't kick a football. That got my hormones pumping to the point where I asked Katherine to go steady. For about a year, she thought I was wonderful. That was grade 11. Grade 11 was a vintage year for my masculinity. I was winning!

I went to a "men's lib" event recently. Most of us were trying to come to terms with that competitive drive inside us, the energy that both empowers and kills us. Most of us really wanted to learn how to be more cooperative. We spent the weekend competing with each other to prove how non-competitive we were.

It's a good thing there were no women present. They would have laughed their heads off.

When I get together with my male friends, I compete with them to tell the latest joke, to know more than almost anyone about whatever we're discussing, to subtly mention just how hard I work and all the great stuff I'm doing. I learned those skills quite well as a kid. And those are skills you don't lose as you get older.

So here I am, a writer. Publisher. I often get invited to make speeches. Or to preach. And all because, as a teenager, I had the athletic ability of drunken dinosaur.

That's why I became a nerd. A successful nerd. I had found a different way to be competitive—to be a man.

Our story

Thou shalt not lose!

The greatest religious festival is not Easter.
Or Christmas.

The greatest religious festivals are the Grey Cup, the Superbowl, the World Series, the Stanley Cup, the World Soccer Championship.

OK, that sounds a little crazy, but think of it this way. Whatever is most important in our lives, that's our religion.

How many people go to church at Christmas or Easter, and how much money do they put on the plate? How many people go to football games on New Year's day and how much do they spend for tickets?

That's right. The faithful flock to the holy temple for the holiest of our high festivals, where they will honor the holy Prophet Vince Lombardi who declared unto the faithful: "Winning isn't everything. It's the only thing." St. Vincent thus articulated the first and only commandment of the faithful. "Thou shalt not lose. Ever." (Losers get dropped from the lineup, then from the team, and finally from life itself as they spend their years as couch potatoes drinking beer and watching sports on TV.)

> *Don't you know that in a race the runners all compete, but only one receives the prize? Run in such a way that you may win it.*
>
> St. Paul
> 1 Corinthians 9:24

I pushed his button

I did a piece on this for the CBC radio network, one year. I talked about the player priests, the sacred rule book. I said the cheer leaders were the vestal virgins (which may have been stretching the truth just a bit). I talked about the Hall of Fame where the saints were enshrined. And I talked about the sports commentators as the theologians of the cult.

The network played my piece to one of Canada's best known sportscasters and asked for his reaction. He was so mad, he could hardly talk. I guess I pushed his button, which may mean that I was more accurate than I'd imagined.

King David and his folks went on wars, and when they won, they came home feeling great, and very worthwhile, and very masculine. We have sport, which is ritualized warfare. Sure it is. That's why the fans yell, "Kill 'em." And in hockey, fans still stand up to see the action when the enforcer on the team throws down his gloves and feeds the other guy a knuckle sandwich. We love it when there's blood on the ice.

Sports may be a healthy outlet for the adrenalin in young bodies. Unfortunately, the couch potatoes in front of the TV get churned up watching, but they don't know what to do with the aggressive instincts this brings out in them. So they take it out on whoever is handy. Superbowl Sunday is the day of the highest reported incidence of child and women abuse in both Canada and the USA. The booze promoted on TV and consumed by the viewers doesn't help the situation.

War is getting to be a spectator sport too. The Vietnam war was the first war fought on TV. The battle with Iraq was as much a media event as a war. During the Iraq war, the generals spent as much time managing the media as they did running the war. The real battle was fought on CNN and Newsworld.

Keeping score

It's the winning that's important. The kings of the world—not the ones with crowns but the guys who run the multinationals—are really not in business at all. They don't need the money. Their incentive has nothing to do with earning a living. It's a game, and money is just how you keep score.

There is, I'm convinced, something about the male psyche that needs to struggle against something. We need to test ourselves, to go, to do, and most often we do that in a physical way. If that's not possible, we'll find another way.

Often that's in competition. Competing in the arts, competing in sports, is just a sophisticated version of the animal mating competition. A couple of guys arm wrestling in a pub are doing the same thing as a couple of bull elks butting heads during the rutting season. Except the human rutting season lasts all year.

Some people say that male brains are hard-wired to be competitive with other males. Competitiveness is there in our bones, they say. I don't think that's necessarily so. I think we are hard-wired to be active, to express our energy, to be aggressive in either the best or worst sense of that word. Some of my feminist friends say this aggressiveness is bad. It's destructive. At its worst it can be downright murderous. And they are right.

But the instinct is still there, whether we want it to be or not. As men, we don't have that choice. It's not a psychological condition we can think or train our way out of. The energy is in the juices that run all through our bodies. And it is reinforced by just about everything we encounter in society and on the media.

That male energy, whatever you want to call it, is both good and bad. Using this aggressiveness, males have fought for justice, invented life-giving medicine, produced beautiful music and showed us the other side of the moon. Male energy can help us be the best of fathers to our children and the finest husbands to our wives.

But that same male energy has also brought starvation and despair, the arms race, huge deposits of excess wealth in a few hands, and violent death to many women, many children, and many other men.

We can dam up a river, but if we don't give the water some place to go, it'll burst over the dam and destroy everything in its path.

Sports into perspective

One of my favorite recreations is watching sports on TV. Hockey and football are my favorites. Both of them are heavy contact sports.

I often squirm while I'm watching. That's probably good. It helps if I watch with a lively sense of humor, recognizing that while those guys on TV are busy being heroes, they are also making asses of themselves. And I'm an ass for watching. It's a high-tech rutting ritual. Hanging loose and having a good laugh brings a lot of things, especially sports, into perspective.

A good laugh also to keep us from despair when we mess up— when once again we fail to understand our energy, when we don't know who we are as men, how we feel, and how we live with people and with the world around us. Our maleness trips us up, over and over.

As a boy, I remember stories about a neighbor who bought a fine horse from some guys in the city. Beautiful beast. It looked just great pulling a buggy down the road. Except that it had been trained to run the steeple chase, and whenever it came to a gate or a fence, it would speed up and jump. The neighbor landed buckboard over backside in the ditch. Jumping is not helpful when you're pulling a buggy.

There's nothing wrong with being male. Let's celebrate the strength and energy that gives us. But let's not go leaping over fences when we should be opening gates.

I've leaped over more than my share of fences and hurt the people I love most. Because I'm slightly smarter than our neighbor's horse (I hope) I can learn from my own mistakes. I think I'm learning that it's better to channel my aggressive energy into cooperation rather than competition. It's far more fun, far more satisfying, to stop and open the gate and walk through together.

High-octane gas

Men have something that the bull elks don't have. Human intelligence. We don't have to be victims of our testosterone. We can use it creatively. History gives us lots of examples to learn from.

I have this fantasy that a couple of million years ago, some poor guy didn't have the muscle to win any wrestling matches, or maybe he was just a lousy shot when it came to throwing spears. At any rate, he had to put his energy somewhere. One day he invented the wheel and became the father of modern technology. (I know, it could just as easily have been a woman who invented the wheel, but that's my fantasy.)

Genghis Khan, Socrates, Julius Caesar, Paul of Tarsus, Michaelangelo, Napoleon, Stalin, Gandhi, Einstein, Martin Luther King, Jr., Jean Vanier, Bill Clinton, you and I—we are all running our engines on the same kind of high-octane gas.

We get to choose where it takes us.

Your story

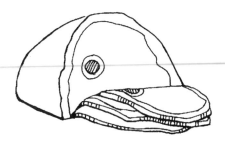

**Questions to discuss,
think about,
or write about**

- Who was your greatest hero when you were 8 years old? When you were 13? When you were 18?
- Who is your greatest hero now?
- How have your heros changed over the years?
- Did you ever dream of being a sports hero? What was your dream?
- In the place where you work, in what way are the men competitive with each other? How are they competitive in church?

- Do you consider yourself competitive? Who do you compete with?
- Do you watch competitive sports on TV? What does it do to you or for you?
- King David was highly competitive. Was that good or bad? Is your own competitiveness good or bad?

Chapter 2

Men want to be "somebody"

David's story

Part II
from fugitive to king-in-waiting

*A loose paraphrase of selected portions of
1 Samuel:
Chapters 21–22
Chapters 24–31.*

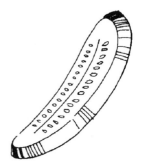

David was on the run. A political refugee. He headed for the town of
Nob where he knew Ahimelech, a priest.

"What's happening?" Ahimelech wanted to know. "David, how
come you're all by yourself?"

Obviously Ahimelech didn't know that David was in trouble with
King Saul, and David wasn't about to tell him.

"Ah," said David. "Listen, I'm on a top-secret mission for the king,
so just don't tell anyone I'm here."

"Really?" Ahimelech was impressed.

"Got anything to eat?"

Out of the corner of his eye, David spotted Doeg walking by. David
had never liked Doeg, a kind of greasy manipulator he simply couldn't
trust. But it didn't occur to him that Doeg was a mole, one of Saul's
spies, using a shepherding job as a front.

"Do you have a sword I could borrow?" David asked Ahimelech.

"You don't have a sword? You never go out without your sword,
David."

"I know, but I was in such a rush to leave, it slipped my mind.

Couldn't you loan me something?"

"Say, I just remembered. David, the sword you took from Goliath? You chopped of his head with it. Remember?"

David nodded. He wasn't likely to forget. The thought occurred to him, "How come I was so brave then when I'm so scared now?" He smiled casually at Ahimelech to cover up the knot in his belly.

"Well, that sword is wrapped up in a cloth at the back of the closet. I guess it's yours as much as any body's."

"Great," said David, taking it. "But look, I've got to split. Thanks for everything." And David was off down the road, with Ahimelech still wondering what was going on.

"Verrrry interesting," said Doeg to himself. "I think King Saul's going to find this very interesting."

David was learning to think on his feet. He was developing the instincts of a street fighter, able to respond quickly to whatever happened.

David decided the best thing to do was to get out of Saul's country altogether. There really wasn't a safe place anywhere in Israel for him. Best to head for Gath.

But the folks in Gath recognized David right off. They ran to tell King Achish. "Guess who's here? King David of Israel."

"Come on!" said King Achish. "Saul is king of Israel."

"For now, sure," said the folks from Gath, "but you know what they say:

> *Saul has whopped a thousand,*
> *But David's whopped ten thousand.*

It's only a matter of time."

"Welcome, King David," said Achish to David.

As soon as he heard that, David knew he was in trouble. If he accepted Achish's greeting, the word would get back to Saul, and Saul would be sure David was trying to replace him. And if he didn't, he was a nobody without any protection.

Again, David felt the knot of fear. Besides, learning to think on his feet, David had become a pretty good actor to boot. So right away he put a weird look on his face and rolled his eyes up in his head. He drooled all over his beard and fell to the floor twitching.

"Get this idiot out of here," said King Achish. "I've got enough nut cases of my own in Gath. King of Israel. Hah!"

They tossed David out of the country, and David ran off into the wilderness and hid in a cave. The fear now was worse than any fear he'd ever known. He was alone and down and out and hungry. David was desperate.

Through all the time in Saul's court, David hardly gave his parents or his family at home a thought. Now he had nowhere else to turn. The cave wasn't far from his folks' place in Bethlehem, and somehow David managed to send word: "Please help me!" When the family found the cave and brought him food, David realized how much he needed them and loved them.

Gradually things began to come together a bit for David. David discovered a few other folks living with him in that cave, all of them in trouble with the law. Eventually the little band grew until there were 400 people in David's group. Most of them were from his own tribe, Judah. And David, being a natural leader, was soon the one in charge.

Which was good news and bad news. The good news was that David was no longer all alone. The bad news was that you can't keep a gathering of 400 folks a secret.

David was now even more of a threat to Saul. Saul's tribe was called Benjamin. The Benjaminites and David's tribe, Judah, tolerated each other at best. Usually. This dust-up between Saul and David didn't help relationships between the two tribes one bit.

Meanwhile, Saul called a meeting of his department heads and a few of the other civil servants around the palace. Including Doeg.

Saul wanted to make a speech. Set a few things straight. "Just in case any of you are thinking of going off and joining that upstart David, just remember which side your bread is buttered on. There's some big promotions coming up in the kingdom, and they'll go to the ones who keep their noses clean.

"Don't all of you look so self-righteous. I know what's been going on around here. My own son, Jonathan, helped him escape, and did any of you tell me about it. Eh? Eh?"

"Ah, sir!" said Doeg. "You might be interested to know that David paid a little visit to the priest Ahimelech. They had a prayer meeting, the two of them. Then Ahimelech gave David some food and Goliath's sword."

"We'll see about that!" said Saul. He sent for the priest, yelled at him for awhile, then had him killed.

That felt good but Saul was still mad. "Send a platoon of soldiers to Nob with orders to kill all the rest of those priests." But the soldiers

wouldn't do it. "Those are God's priests," they said. "We can't just go
and kill them."

"Doeg!!" yelled Saul. Doeg came running. "Doeg, you're the only
one I can trust. You go and terminate those priests. Every damned one
of them."

Doeg wasn't one for half measures. He gathered a group of merce-
naries, headed off to Nob, and killed everybody. Priests, women,
children, animals. Everybody and everything.

Except for Ahitub, one of Ahimelech's sons. He managed to hide in
some bushes and later escaped to tell David.

"Damn!" said David. "I saw Doeg sneaking around when I was
talking to Ahimelech. I should have known he'd tell Saul. It's all my
fault. That whole bloody massacre is my fault."

David sensed this was a turning point. Killing the priests didn't do
much for Saul's popularity, which was pretty low already. More and
more people threw in their lot with David, usually because they were in
trouble with Saul. Sometimes they were being oppressed and perse-
cuted. Some people came because they figured David was going to win
out in the end and they wanted to be on the winning side.

David didn't know how to get back on Saul's good side. Things had
just gone too far for that. But David was totally convinced that God had
anointed Saul king over Israel, and David was determined not to be
responsible for Saul's downfall.

Not that there weren't chances. Saul had 3000 soldiers with him,
trying to find David. David and a few of his men were hiding out in a
cave. Saul and his soldiers stood around right outside trying to figure
out what to do next. They had no idea David and his men were inside.
Saul needed to relieve himself, so he went inside the cave.

"Now's your chance, David," whispered some of the men. But
David just snuck up behind Saul and clipped off a corner of his cloak.

"Jeez," said his men. "You blew it. A perfect chance to kill the old
buzzard."

"God made him king," said David. "It's not my job to unmake him."

But David wasn't above rubbing Saul's nose in it. When Saul's
army was far enough away, David stood up on a rock and yelled, "Hey,
King Saul. Look, at this. It's a piece of your cloak. I chopped it off
while you were in the cave having a tinkle. I could have cut your throat
just as easily. So why do you keep telling everybody I'm after your
hide? I don't want your job. Why do you waste your time chasing me?"

That hit Saul right where he lived. For a few moments of reality, Saul realized he was pretty paranoid about David. "I'm sorry, David, my son," said Saul. "I've been a total jerk. I'm sorry."

David accepted the apology, but he knew it wouldn't last. He'd been through all this before. So David and his men went back to hiding out in the hills.

David had enough followers now to be a kind of traveling town, but they had no way of raising any food of their own. David became a warlord, a bit of a "Robin Hood" fighting on behalf of the poor. At least, that's how his friends described him. Others said David was running a plain old protection racket.

"There's a rich guy over in Carmel," David said to ten of his men. "Go over and see if you can get him to make a contribution to our work."

"Hi there, Nabal," said David's men. "How's everything? How's the little woman?"

"Never mind her. What do you guys want?"

"David, our leader, says to say hello. We hear things are going pretty well for you. Lots of sheep. Lots of good crops. We'd just like to point out that nobody has bothered you for a long time. Nobody has stolen anything. That's because we've been keeping an eye on your stuff for you, Nabal."

"What do you guys want?" Nabal snarled at them.

"Well, you know Nabal, it takes a lot of folks to make sure nothing gets stolen from you. We were wondering if you could help out a little with the groceries. You know. Anything lying around you can spare."

"Who are you protecting me from?" said Nabal. "From that gang of punks David's collected! David wants me to pay him for not stealing from me? You go tell David to take his protection and shove it in his ear!"

David was not amused. He strapped on his sword and called to his men, "All right guys. I think it's time we taught Nabal a few manners."

When Nabal's wife Abigail heard about this from one of the servants, she sounded the red alert. "Grab a batch of bread, and some mutton," she yelled. "Load them on the donkey. And some wine, too. Lots of wine. And anything else you can lay your hands on. If Nabal hasn't got enough horse sense to save our skins, I'll do it for him."

So Abigail and servants and donkeys loaded with grub set out to find David. David meanwhile was on his way to find Nabal. Fortunately they met on the road.

"Please, David," said Abigail. "Don't take Nabal seriously. He didn't really mean it. He's pretty stupid and he's been under a lot of stress. Look, I brought you a whole mess of food, and some great wine. Here. Try some. See? And there's more where that came from."

David was both surprised and impressed. "You are one sharp lady," said David. "So, okay. Tell your hubby you saved his bacon."

Abigail told Nabal the morning after a big party when his head was pounding like a football after a 50-yard field goal. Nabal had a fit when he realized how close he'd come to disaster. The fact that he had been saved by a woman did his male ego no good at all. Nabal went into shock. Ten days later, he was dead.

David had been surprised and impressed by Abigail. "Serves him right," said David when he heard that Nabal had died. "Proves I was right and he was wrong." So David sent one of his assistants to Abigail to tell her, "I want you for my wife."

"Do I have a choice?" asked Abigail. She didn't need an answer.

David also married Ahinoam, so he had two wives. As for Michal, who had been his wife before Saul got on his case, well Saul gave her away to a guy named Palti.

"Do I have a choice?" Michal wondered to herself. She didn't even bother asking the question out loud.

Saul meanwhile, was on the hunt again with the same 3000 select troops. David had his own spies out, who told him exactly where Saul was and what was going on.

"I need a volunteer," said David. "Anyone want to go and sneak into Saul's camp at night? Just for a bit of fun."

Abishai put up his hand. "I'll go."

So David and Abishai waited until the middle of the night when everyone in Saul's camp was totally zonked out from a hard day's marching and a bit too much wine. David and Abishai walked right into the middle of the camp, right into Saul's tent. There was Saul, snoring away, with his water jug beside him and his spear stuck in the ground.

Abishai signaled to David to let him use Saul's own spear to kill him right on the spot. But David replied thumbs down on that idea. Instead, he picked up the water jug and tugged the spear out of the ground and the two of them snuck back out of the camp.

"Thank God they didn't wake up!" said Abishai.

"God put them to sleep for us," said David.

"But why didn't you let me pin Saul to the ground with his own

spear?" asked Abishai. "I could have done it quickly and quietly."

"When God decides it's time for Saul to die, then God will do what is necessary," said David. "I'm not going to have Saul's death on my head."

In the morning, David went to a hillside across the valley from Saul's camp. He started yelling for Abner, the commander-in-chief of Saul's troops.

"Abner! Wake up, dozer. Did you have a good snooze Abner? Did you know that we were walking around the middle of your camp last night? We could have killed Saul real easy. It's your job to protect the king, Abner. You flunked out. You know what that means, Abner? There's the death penalty for not protecting the king."

"Is that you, David?" Saul had heard the yelling and came out of his tent rubbing his eyes."

"Yes, it's me, King Saul. And I want to know why you keep chasing me. What have I done? Who's telling you lies about me? And why do you bring 3000 guys out here to chase down one man? It doesn't make any sense."

"I've done it again, David," Saul called back. "I'm sorry, and I promise not to hurt you. Ever. Come back home David. I've been pretty stupid, but I promise not to make the same mistake."

David held up Saul's spear. "Here's your spear, Saul. Send one of your men up here to get it. I was in your tent last night. I've got your spear and your water jug."

"Bless you David, my son!" called Saul. "You are a fair and honest man. You'll do well in life. I know you will."

Of course, David knew better than to take up Saul's invitation to go back to the palace. In fact, David was getting a little tired of running around Judah trying to stay a few steps ahead of Saul. So David took his traveling town, 600 men, lots of them with wives and children, and headed for the country of the Philistines.

David struck a deal with Achish, one of the warlords of the area known as Gath. (Gath was actually where big Goliath had come from.) Presumably David managed to convince Achish that the madness on his earlier visit was just a bad case of 24-hour flu. Or maybe having 600 soldiers with him changed the relationship a little. At any rate, Achish gave him the town of Ziklag, right near the border of Judah. David moved in with the whole kit and caboodle of his traveling town.

It was a good location. From there, David could go out on raids to various towns in Judah. David had an efficient way of making sure nobody started spreading stories about him being just another punk who went around stealing stuff and killing people. When David raided a town, he killed everybody. Everybody. That way there was nobody left to spread stories.

Achish became convinced that David's reputation in Judah was shot. "I've got that guy in my pocket!" said Achish. "He's got nowhere to go." So he decided to use David and his fighters as his personal bodyguard.

Meanwhile, Saul and his company got into yet another fight with the Philistines. The whole war began to focus around a battle shaping up in Gilboa.

It didn't look good for Saul and the army of Israel. "I need some advice!" Saul said. So he tried praying, but God wouldn't answer. The line had gone dead.

"Can't you find me a fortuneteller or something?" he asked one of his servants.

"Well, sir," said the servant. "You outlawed them. You said, 'No more witches or mediums or fortunetellers.'"

"Find me one anyway!" Saul wasn't in a mood for arguments.

Saul disguised himself to look like one of his foot soldiers. In the middle of the night, the servant took Saul to a woman in Endor.

"Can you help me?" said Saul. "I need to talk to a guy whose been dead for awhile, and I understand you can help me make contact."

"Not on your life!" said the woman. "It's against the law. You're just trying to trick me. I know your type."

"No. Honest. Nothing will happen to you, I promise."

Finally, he convinced the woman. "I need to talk with Samuel, the prophet." And sure enough, with appropriate incantations and smoke and mirrors, the woman brought in the spirit of Samuel.

But as soon as she saw that spirit starting to materialize, the penny dropped. "You're King Saul!" she yelled.

"Relax," said Saul. "Just tell me what you see."

"I see an old geezer coming up, wrapped in an old robe."

"That's him," said Saul.

"What are you bothering me for?" Samuel's ghost wanted to know.

"I'm in deep trouble," said Saul. "The Philistines are all set to fight us, but I can't get any response out of God so I don't know what's going to happen or what I should do."

"So why do you ask me? God is mad at you because you didn't do as you were told. Which means the Philistines are going to skin you alive tomorrow. You haven't got a hope. Over and out."

Samuel's ghost disappeared and Saul rolled on the ground absolutely scared spitless. The servant was shaking in his boots. The only one doing any thinking was the woman, who said, "I'll get you something to eat. That'll make you feel better." So she made Saul a roast beef sandwich. That helped. But not much.

The Philistine troops were also getting ready for the big battle. Achish even had David and his followers there to help out. Achish was comfortable with David fighting on the Philistine side, but it didn't sit well with the other Philistine generals.

"You know what'll happen?" the generals said to Achish. "Just when we get to the tough part of the battle, when the Israelites are hacking away at our front lines, David will decide he's really on their side and start hacking at our backsides. Get rid of him."

"Sorry, David," said Achish. "I think you're OK, but the generals don't trust you. Go back to Ziklag. We'll try again some other time."

Which was just as well, because when David and his boys got back to Ziklag, there was nobody home. Not only that, the whole place was trashed. Somebody had done to them what David had been doing to other towns and villages, only David found it wasn't as much fun being done to as it was doing.

Besides, David's own men were flaming mad. A few of them started to pick up rocks to throw at him. "You get us off fighting for those Philistines who don't want us anyway, and we lose our families and our homes in the process." It was not a happy scene.

David was a pretty good talker as well as a good fighter. So he screwed up his courage and talked them down out of their anger. Then he had a conversation with God. "So should I chase after whoever it was that did this?" he asked.

"Go for it!" said God.

So David took his 600 men, who were already played out after marching back and forth between Ziklag and the Philistine army. After another day or so of marching, about 200 of them just couldn't move another muscle. "Stay here," said David. "We'll pick you up on the way back."

Eventually they found a man wandering around in the wilderness. He was starved and dehydrated and generally in pretty rough shape. They gave him something to eat and drink, and it turned out he'd been left behind by the folks who had attacked Ziklag.

"OK," said David, "you have a choice. You can lead us to your raiding party, or we'll slice you up and leave you to the vultures." It didn't take the man long to consider the alternatives.

They found the raiding party, a bunch of Amalekites, having a big party with all the stuff they'd stolen from Ziklag and various other places. David and his men swooped down on them, hacking and slicing with swords. A few of the Amalekites managed to climb on their camels and run, but David killed most of them.

They saved all the women and children, including Abigail and Ahinoam. And all their stuff. David and his men also grabbed the loot the Amalekites had lifted from other towns and villages—gold and silver and cattle—but nobody suggested they turn that in to the local Lost and Found. David was pretty proud of himself.

> Over a period of fifteen years [David Rothenberge] talked with thousands of adults and teenage male criminal offenders, and found "an amazing similarity" in their explanations of what led them to commit crimes: "I wanted them to know that I was no sissy" and "I had to prove that I was a man" were among the most frequent explanations given."
>
> Myriam Miedzian
> *Boys Will Be Boys*
> Doubleday, 1991

Normally, all that booty would be divided among the troops who took part in the actual fighting. But when they got to the 200 guys who were too pooped to go any further, David changed the rules. "They did their best," he said. "So they get their share, same as everybody."

"Just a damn minute," said the guys who had walked the whole way and done the fighting. "They sat here on their duffs, while we risked our necks. No fair."

"They did their best. They get a share same as everybody. So shut up."

Through all this, David was thinking ahead to his own future and decided on a foxy political move. He sent some of the loot from the Amalekites as gifts to the movers and shakers in Judah. "Doesn't hurt to make a few friends," said David.

Meanwhile, the Philistines were having their way with Saul's army. It was a pretty grizzly affair. Jonathan was killed. When Saul saw that it was all over, he killed himself. Just as Samuel's ghost had predicted, it was a rout. The Philistines took Saul's and Jonathan's bodies and hung them from the wall of their city. The bodies would have stayed there for the buzzards to eat, except that a few of the survivors in Saul's army did the brave and decent thing. They cut the bodies down, and brought them home for cremation and burial.

My story

When I grow up...

"What are your career objectives?" the personnel manager wanted to know.

I didn't have any career objectives. I needed a job, that's all. "Stupid question," I thought.

I got the job as office boy with a paint company. After a few weeks I knew that my career objectives included not working for that company. I won a contest and got a job as a radio announcer, which I hung on to for the three-month probation period. Then I was told I could either move to Saskatoon or quit. Preferably quit. I went to the radio station in Saskatoon and lasted long enough there to learn a little about the job.

Ah, those were the days in Saskatoon. A brand new radio station, with a staff of kids really. Not one of us was much over 30. I was almost 18 and looked old enough to get into the beer parlor, which I did fairly often. The beer parlor was an all-male preserve in those days.

"I'm not staying in this burg for long," I boasted. "How long do
y'figure before a guy can hit the big time?

"Speaking of the big time," I went on, "Did you see the redhead
they hired as a receptionist? You could have a big time with that chick,
I bet. Looks as if she really wants it."

The "chick's" name was Ida, and I took her to a movie, then tried to
get invited up to her apartment. She said, "No."

"What do you mean, 'No'?" I asked.

"Just 'No'," she said.

That's not the story I told the guys in the beer parlor, of course.

A few days later I had coffee with Ida. "I want to go back to
school," she said. "I want to be a nurse."

"Why?" I asked. "Nurses don't make any money."

"Because God wants me to."

"Is that why you wouldn't...ah?"

"Yes."

I had no idea what she was talking about. But her comment bugged
me and kept me awake at night. Why would she give up fun and money
because God wanted her to. "Stupid idea," I thought. "Who believes in
God, anyway?"

Yet I admired her for that and wished I had that kind of gumption.
And I felt guilty because I'd told the guys I'd gone to bed with her,
which didn't make a bit of sense because I knew the guys didn't believe
me anyway.

Several years later, in Calgary—déja vu. This time her name was
Janet, she was already a nurse, and I asked her to marry me.

She said no too. "God wants me to go overseas as a missionary.
That's why I trained to be a nurse."

Missionary! How can anybody be so stupid—to turn me down to
become a missionary! And yet I admired Janet too, and kind of envied
her conviction. But a missionary? For the church?

In the meantime, I was becoming pretty good at my trade, enjoying
the "fame," such as it was, and becoming known as a bit of a jock.
Along the way, I ran the very first open-line talk show in Canada,
which didn't hurt my ego one bit.

And then there was May. May turned out to be the kind of woman
the guys thought Ida was, except that May was "a couple of sandwiches
short of a picnic" and really didn't understand the consequences. She
knocked on my door one day, just walked in and sat on my bed. I could

tell she had been drinking. And just in time the question formed in my head. "Is this right? She is a child in a woman's body. Is this right?" And I backed off. She eventually went home angry and insulted and muttering remarks about my masculinity.

Late that night I wondered. Was I being noble or simply scared? Who was I protecting—May or myself? Both probably, and I wondered whether God could speak to people through fear. That thought surprised me because at that time I didn't believe there was a God.

> *Seek and you shall find.*
> Jesus
> Matthew 7:7
> and Luke 11:9

The God I didn't believe in kept asking questions—became a burr under my britches—until one day when I was dressed up in a rented tux, portable tape recorder in hand, knocking on doors asking women if they had Robin Hood Flour in the house. If they said "Yes," I gave them a silver dollar and they talked into my tape machine about how wonderful Robin Hood Flour was. If they said "No," I thanked them and left. The whole exercise seemed to be utterly stupid, and I felt angry and humiliated by it all.

That's when God popped the question. It came through a child hanging on to the skirt of a woman who had Robin Hood Flour in the house. "What are you?" the child wanted to know.

What am I? Good question. By this time I had begun to realize that God's best questions are asked through the most unlikely people at the oddest times.

Fifteen years later, I happened to meet Janet again—the nurse who wanted to be a missionary. She had married and settled down to raise a house full of children. In the meantime, I had married Bev and we had gone to the Philippines as—you won't believe this—missionaries!

Our story

How to be a wimp

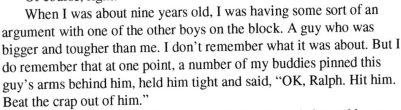

"Son, I'd like you to grow up to be a
real wimp!"
 What kind of a dad would say that
to his son? A man should be a man,
right?
 Of course, right.
 When I was about nine years old, I was having some sort of an
argument with one of the other boys on the block. A guy who was
bigger and tougher than me. I don't remember what it was about. But I
do remember that at one point, a number of my buddies pinned this
guy's arms behind him, held him tight and said, "OK, Ralph. Hit him.
Beat the crap out of him."
 I didn't. And I can't tell you now whether I was being noble, or
whether I was scared he'd get back at me as soon as my buddies were
gone.
 What I didn't know was that my Dad saw the whole thing. That
night, when I was lying on my bed, he came to me, sat down, and said,
"Son, I was very proud of you today. That was a very brave thing to do.
It took a great deal of courage not to hit that boy. That's the mark of a
real man."
 Was my old man telling me to be a wimp? Well, if I look in my
dictionary, it defines a wimp as a "week, ineffectual or insipid person."
 OK, let's look up the word, "manly." It says, "Not effeminate or
timorous, bold, resolute and open in conduct or bearing; of undaunted
courage." But my dad said I'd been very brave. So was I a wimp or was
I manly?
 Here's the big problem. From the time we can walk till we reach
our second childhood, we are told in a zillion ways that we've got to be
manly. Real men. Tough. Resolute. We don't back down from nothin',
see! And we will do almost anything to prove this, especially insulting
or beating any male who thinks or says otherwise. It is a key element in
our social survival that nobody finds out how scared we really are.
 Do you know why President Lyndon B. Johnson got the Americans
up to their eyebrows in the Vietnam war? Here's a direct quote: "We've

got to show the world whose got the biggest balls."

There's a terrible cost for boys and men who think or feel otherwise. Losing a fight is bad, but running away from a fight would have the other kids yelling "Scaredy Cat" at you. Boys who refuse to "take the man" in hockey are benched. Teenage boys who don't try to be jocks are called "nerds" and "wimps" and "fruits." It takes courage for a teenage boy to be interested in girls as people, instead of chicks available for him to lay. It takes even more strength for him to admit that to his friends.

A young man starting out in the business world is under tremendous pressure to play the game according to the rules of Madison Avenue and Wall Street. A young man who refuses a dishonest deal or turns down a job because he feels such work should not be done, or puts the needs of people ahead of his concern for profit, just won't succeed, according to the values he sees in the beer commercials. It takes guts to stand up for your convictions and let your friends call you a wimp.

And yet there are such men. Strong men who show their strength by caring for other people, by struggling for what is right rather than for what is profitable.

Webster's dictionary is wrong. The guys they call "wimps" are often men who refuse to be intimidated by their peers. They think their own thoughts and know who they are. They are ready to swim up stream. The guys who are tough and resolute, who show courage and inner strength, these are strong guys who get called "wimps."

It's easy to run with the pack, so everybody thinks you're a jock, even though deep down inside you want badly to be your own authentic self. It takes metal to stand up on your own hind legs, think your own thoughts, have your own convictions and be the man God calls you to be even when that is unpopular.

So guys! Let's hear it for the wimps. They've got what it takes to be real men.

Your story

**questions to discuss,
think about,
or write about**

- What pressures were you under in your teens and early 20s? Can you recall any instances where what you believed ran against popular opinion?
- What were your "career objectives" then? What are your "career objectives" now?
- Did you identify with David when he was hiding out in the cave behind Bethlehem? Have you ever been "hiding out" at any point in your life?
- Did you identify with David when he was a popular warlord? Have you ever been involved in dealings you are not completely proud of?
- What did you feel like when you were a young man with your whole adult life ahead of you? Would you have called yourself a "wimp" or a "jock?"

Chapter 3

Men work

David's story

Part III
**from rookie king
to successful monarch**

*A loose paraphrase based on 2 Samuel:
Chapter 1:1-2:4,
Chapter 3:1,
Chapter 3:26-5:16,
Chapter 6:1-7:18,
Chapter 8:1,
Chapter 8:13-8:14,
Chapter 9:1-9:8
Chapter 11:1*

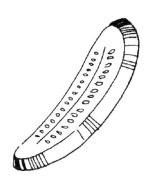

It was three days after David and his men came back from thrashing the Amalekites. David couldn't get his mind off the battle between the Israelites and the Philistines. He knew it must be decided by now.

Then a man came running into the camp looking as if someone had dragged him through a meat grinder. "I managed to get away," the man gasped, "but I don't think anyone else did."

"So what happened? Talk!" yelled David.

"It was bloody awful," the man moaned. "The whole Israelite army is on the run. King Saul and his son Jonathan were killed."

"Oh God, no!" cried David. "How do you know that? Are you sure?"

"Positive. I came to the top of Mount Gilboa, trying to get away from the real dirty fighting. There was King Saul...he was leaning into his spear, trying to kill himself. He called me over and told me, 'Hurry it up,' he said. 'Kill me. The Philistines are just over the hill, and I don't want to be alive when they get here. Hurry up. Finish me off.' So I did it. I mean, it was an order from the king, right? What could I do? Then I took the crown off his head, and I brought it here to you, sir."

Well, David began to wail and to cry. He doubled up in pain and tore at his clothes. "Kill that bastard!" he yelled, pointing at the man who brought the bad news. "Kill him. He murdered the man God appointed king."

David was totally broken up over Saul, but especially over his friend Jonathan. Some of his people were getting worried, his grief was so deep and so violent. But time brought David relief from the first waves of frantic grief. And then David found better ways to mourn, ways that brought with them some healing.

As he often did at times of high emotion, David wrote a poem:

> *The beauty of Israel lies dead on the hill.*
> *Oh, how have the mighty fallen!*
> *You hills of Gilboa...*
> *there'll be no dew or rain for you,*
> *because you have taken the life of Saul,*
> *the king God sent for Israel.*
> *Saul and Jonathan were good people,*
> *real men,*
> *who died bravely like eagles and lions.*
> *Oh, how have the mighty fallen!*
> *Jonathan, my friend Jonathan,*
> *you were so good to me.*
> *Your love for me was wonderful,*
> *more wonderful than any woman I have known.*
> *Oh, how have the mighty fallen!*

Eventually, David realized that with Saul dead, there was no more reason to hide away in the land of the Philistines. So David asked God, "Should I go back to Judah?"

"Go," said God.

"Can you be more specific?"

"Hebron," said God.

"Abigail! Ahinoam!" yelled David. "Start packing. We're heading home."

So David and his wives, and all the roughneck fighters and their families, and the whole portable town, packed up and headed back to

Judah. And the folks in Judah were glad to see him back. So glad, that by popular demand they made David the king of Judah.

But not king over Saul's tribe of Benjamin, or any of the tribes of Israel. Abner, who had been Saul's commander-in-chief, brought Saul's son Isbaal and set him up as king of Israel. So the country was divided, Israel in the north and Judah in the south.

Then it started. The power politics. The sneaky plans. The lies. The murders. David and his supporters tried to get control of Israel. Isbaal and Abner tried desperately to hang on to power, but they seemed to lose one round after another. David had all the moves.

Eventually Abner turned against Isbaal in a quarrel over one of Isbaal's wives. Abner joined up with David, but Joab, David's second-in-command, figured Abner wasn't sincere, so he ordered him killed. David was pretty mad about that, or at least pretended to be, and executed the guys who did it. Not Joab, of course. Just the guys who had followed orders. Abner had been very popular in the north, so being outraged by his murder was a good political move.

When Isbaal got the news that Abner was dead, he went into a tailspin. He couldn't keep his guard up and so it wasn't long before he too was assassinated. David made a big fuss over that too, saying it wasn't right that Isbaal had been killed. David showed all sorts of public grief over the murder and had the goons who pulled it off executed.

In the process, David got Michal back. Her second husband wasn't thrilled, but he really wasn't in a position to argue. Neither was Michal. She felt like a political pawn, and that's exactly what she was.

Among many things, David was a smart politician. He worked hard at being king and his schemes worked. He seemed to do all the right things at the right time with the right folks. David had a strong intuitive streak, but he also worked hard gathering information and thinking through his actions. When necessary, he could make a quick, intuitive decision. Eventually, all the tribes of Israel got together and decided that David should be king of Israel as well as Judah.

"Who, me?" said David, trying hard to look surprised.

Israel was one nation again and David was the king. Not bad for a shepherd kid just 30 years old. Not bad in days when the life expectancy of kings was pretty short. By then, David had been king of Judah for seven years; he would be king over all Israel for another 33 years. For the first time in its painful history, the tiny nation enjoyed some stability.

David knew he'd have to work hard to keep this nation together.

The country needed a capital city. David organized an expedition against Jerusalem, the one city in the area that was still held by the Jebusites, the folks who had lived in the area before the Israelites took the country away from them. Jerusalem didn't belong to either Israel or Judah, and was right on the border between them. It was a perfect capital to unite the country.

Jerusalem was well defended, with high walls all around. In fact, the Jebusites bragged that nobody could take the city. But David sent his men up a long water shaft into the center of the city one night, so they opened its gates from the inside, and David's troops poured in. That little exploit had the guys in the pubs talking for years, and didn't do David's reputation any harm.

So David moved in and fixed it all up, and everybody was more or less happy. He built himself a nice house out of cedar to live in. (Things have always been different in Israel—then, as now, the poor folks had stone houses, and the rich ones had wood.)

But David figured his personal image needed some work. So he got himself a bunch of concubines, women who had even fewer rights than wives, if that was possible. Between them and at least three wives (Abigail, Ahinoam and now Michal again—probably more than 20 women in all), David was a busy man. Soon there were a bunch of kids. That didn't hurt David's reputation with the jocks in the pubs who entertained themselves many a night sniggering at his sexual exploits. For David, it was just part of the job.

> *Please, lead a life worthy of your call to a vocation.*
> Ephesians 4:1

Then David took his army out for a couple of good rounds against the Philistines and trounced them. David was riding high and doing just fine, but to sustain that, he had to work long hours. Sometimes at night, as he lay on his bed trying to get to sleep, he felt desperately tired and lonely.

Jerusalem was now the military and political capital of the nation, but David was also convinced that God was directing his life and the life of his nation. David had a deep and personal relationship with God. So he decided to bring the Ark of the Covenant into Jerusalem, to turn Jerusalem the political capital into Jerusalem the holy city.

The Ark was the most important religious symbol of the northern tribes. Wherever the Ark was, they figured that's where God was too. God was everywhere, but God was particularly present in the Ark.

For David, this felt like the most important moment in his life. He took his whole army, 30,000 soldiers, to parade the Ark down the road to Jerusalem. They put it on a brand new cart, and David with his whole entourage danced and sang in front of it. It was quite a festival.

But Murphy's Law worked in David's day too. Uzzah, one of the priests walking beside the ark, reached out to steady the ark when the oxen jerked the cart...Zap! He was dead as a doornail.

"Time out!" yelled David. "This Ark is too hot to handle." He turned to his friend Obed-edom. "Can you take care of the Ark for me while I figure out what to do next?"

A few months later one of his advisors brought David a report. "Obed-edom is having great success with that Ark. Everything works out for him. No matter what he tries, it works."

"Well," said David. "Let's finish the job."

Out came all the soldiers and singers and dancers to see the Ark the rest of the way into Jerusalem. David staged an elaborate religious ceremony followed by a big celebration. David had never felt closer to God, except perhaps during his very first years in the hills above Bethlehem. David danced his joy in front of the whole procession, wearing just a linen ephod, a kind of apron that covered only the front of his body. Sort of. When he wasn't whirling around, that is.

Then everyone went home, including David who didn't know what hit him when he walked in the door.

"So! How's the big man?" Michal was flaming mad. "Did you have fun dancing around stark naked in front of those sweet, innocent girls? Did the great king of Israel enjoy himself, showing his bare buns to all those panting bimbos?"

"Hah!" yelled David. "Who do you think you're talking to? You're just jealous because it's me who's king and not your old man. Well, like it or lump it. Those girls liked what they saw, and I'll

show them even more if I want. But as for you, this is the last you've
seen of me!"

It was a battle Michal couldn't win. David held all the aces. Now
she wouldn't even have children, which was the one thing that gave a
woman any status in those days. Michal lived out her days on the
fringes of the harem while David forgot all about her and went on to
plan his next triumph.

That involved building a temple. When David brought the Ark to
Jerusalem, it dawned on him he had no proper place to put it. So David
called in his top religious advisor, Nathan the prophet.

"It's not right," said David. "I live in this beautiful house, and the
Ark of God sits out there in that drafty old tent."

"So, do whatever you think is best," Nathan shrugged. But that
night Nathan couldn't sleep. David's idea of building a fancy temple
bothered him. The God of his ancestors had never been much for a big
show. Yahweh never seemed much impressed with glitz.

So Nathan went back to David. "Wrong, David. All wrong. God
doesn't want a fancy temple that's got wealth and prosperity written all
over it. God's been moving around with the folks out there in the
wilderness, living in tents, the same as they were. God isn't really all
that comfortable with the rich folks, David. God's really more at home
with the poor.

"So concentrate on building up the house of David, the nation of
Israel, and let somebody else build the house of the Lord. Remember
what kind of a god you worship and you'll do well. You might even get
to be an old man and die in bed, which you've got to admit is pretty
unusual for a king."

David got all choked up. He went into the tent where the Ark of
God was kept and prayed for a long, long time. In the end, David knew
that God wanted him to build up the people of Israel, and leave the
temple for another time. Perhaps for another king.

But all work and no play makes David a dull boy. He decided
another battle with the Philistines would be fun about now. Like the
previous round, this was no contest. Then David took on the Moabites.
Same results. And the Zobah. And the Armeneans. And anyone else
who happened to be nearby. David was a superstar, #1 king of the
whole middle east finishing the war season with a perfect 5-0 record.

David collected tribute (a polite word for extortion) from all those
countries he had beaten. Which meant all the wealth was coming in to

his country and very little was going out—a handy balance-of-payments surplus. So everyone in Israel was doing just fine, financially.

Well, almost everyone. The poor folks were as poor as always. Somehow, the trickle-down theory of wealth distribution never seemed to quite work for them.

David was a good manager. He knew how to handle people. He got his bureaucracy ticking along. In fact, at home David was at the top of the opinion polls. He would have been re-elected by a landslide, but of course, kings don't run for election.

Just because things were going well, David didn't sit on his laurels. Time to do a bit of political fence-mending. The folks in the north still thought of David as a southerner, and felt just a tiny bit sore about how David had become king.

So David called in Ziba, one of Saul's old servants. "Are there any of Saul's people still around? Can you help me find them so that I can show them there's no hard feelings?"

"Your friend Jonathan had a son named Mephibosheth," said Ziba. "He's a cripple. His feet are all twisted up."

So David arranged for Mephibosheth to come to the palace in Jerusalem. Mephibosheth was pretty spooked by the whole process, and wondered if David was set on wiping out the last of King Saul's household.

"Relax," said David. "I don't intend to hurt you. In fact, I'm going to give you back a big slice of what your folks lost. And listen, you can come and live with me here in the palace."

David knew he should be content. He felt blessed by God, though he would often remark to his friends that it took a lot of work to get that blessing. David was the most powerful monarch in that part of the world. Sure, he had put on a bit of weight. Quite a bit of weight in fact. Spicy food gave him heartburn and garlic would have him burping for hours. Lots of nights he would just go to bed without visiting any of his wives or

concubines, but then, even though he was dead tired, he had trouble sleeping.

"Signs of success," he said to himself. "Everything's working out just as I planned." To keep his hand in, David had a small war with the Armeneans, which of course he won easily. But often he would walk around the roof of his beautiful palace, to relieve the tension of a stressful day. He would enjoy the view, and give himself a little mental pat on the shoulder. God had been good to him.

Sometimes David would pick up his lyre and dash off a psalm or two.

> *Bless the Lord, O my soul,*
> *and all that is within me,*
> *bless God's holy name.*

"I've done it," said David. "I've done everything—with God's help of course—everything I ever dreamed of. What more could I possibly want?"

And yet, somehow, it still wasn't enough.

My story

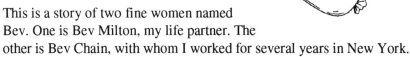

Two Bevs
and the Peter Principle

This is a story of two fine women named
Bev. One is Bev Milton, my life partner. The
other is Bev Chain, with whom I worked for several years in New York.
Bev Chain and I worked in an agency of the National Council of
Churches in the USA. Our particular branch had the ridiculous acronym
of RAVEMCCO. It stood for the Radio, Audio-Visual Education, Mass
Communications Committee, which always struck me as more of a
description than a name.

I was in charge of Operational Research. I was never quite sure
what that meant, but it had something to do with helping churches, most
of them in Africa, to develop communications facilities. It was exciting
work that took me on long trips to Africa, sometimes twice a year, to
say nothing of numerous other trips around the US and Canada. It was
fun and it was challenging. And it was destroying my marriage.

Bev Chain had the office next to mine. It was a good working
relationship for both of us. She had many of the skills I lacked, and vice
versa. Then the heads of our division decided that we should merge
with the literacy development agency down the hall. I was given the job
of working out the merger into what is now known as Intermedia. At
least that was a name, not a description.

The structure I put together was lean and mean and didn't require
cutting any jobs, except those of the two existing directors, both of
whom were within months of retirement. I recommended that a new
director be found for the new merged agency.

"We'd like you to be the Acting Director," the head of our division
said to me. "And we'd like you to apply for the permanent position. Of
course we've got to advertise the position and consider anyone who
applies, but I think you'd be a prime candidate."

I wish I had said, "No. Bev Chain should have the job. She's been
here longer and is more highly qualified." I didn't, and I could see the
pain in her eyes when I told her what was happening. "It should be your
job," I finally blurted out. "It's not fair."

That's when she told me to take the job. "It's just the way things are," Bev Chain argued that day. "I am a woman. You are a man. That means you get the job and I don't. If you turn it down, they'll just get another man. It's unfair," she agreed angrily, "but at least you and I can work together."

I took the job—along with the sense of guilt that it didn't really belong to me. It belonged to Bev Chain. Not only that, I realized it was the "Peter Principle" in spades, where people are promoted beyond the level of their competence.

Well, not quite. I could do the job, but I hated it. When I wasn't attending meetings or flying somewhere, I was at my desk signing my name to the bottom of papers I didn't have time to read. I was a bureaucrat, pure and simple.

At home, things were getting worse. More travel instead of less. And Bev (my spouse) seemed to look more tired, and the kids seemed to be strangers, and I never seemed to know what was going on with any of them.

Bev tried to explain. "The world doesn't stop when you go on a trip. Life goes on even if you're not here. We have to deal with things, and so we begin to function like a single-parent family. But you expect to pick up just where things left off when you got on that airplane. It just doesn't work that way, Ralph."

Barney Luben, the man who had been the Director of RAVEMCCO and taken early retirement at my suggestion, popped in to say hello one day. "How's the job?" he asked.

I'd been asked that question hundreds of times before and always replied with a cheerful, "Fine. Just fine." Wasn't it obvious? I was in a large corner office signing checks for several million dollars, relating to churches on every continent, attending top-level meetings. I had power and prestige and a good, fat, salary. Of course everything was fine. What more could any man want?

But when Barney asked the question this time, nothing seemed to come out of my mouth. Bev Chain had seen Barney coming in, and wanted to say "Hi" to him as well. She walked in just as Barney spoke and she noted my non-response. Gently she closed the door to the outer office.

"This is the wrong job for you, Ralph," she said. "You are a creative doer. You're a writer. A poet. You're no manager. I know you're now in a position to fire me for saying that, but it's true."

I looked at Barney. He nodded. "This is not where God wants you to be," said Barney.

I was upset and angry and changed the subject.

That night I told Bev about that conversation. She said nothing. Her silence spoke volumes and angered me almost as much.

Sitting in the living room later, I was trying to divert my mind by reading the newspaper when our eldest son Mark came along. "I've got some homework, Dad. I'm supposed to write a paragraph about what my Dad does at work."

"Not now, Mark. I'm busy."

I returned to the newspaper which was open at the section titled, "Help Wanted—Male."

Our story

Work, work, work

I have a couple of loose cannons banging around in my head. Snippets of poems that occur to me often—that make me mad because I know I believe them, even when I don't want to. Here's one.

We must be up and doing, aye, each minute.
The grave gives time for rest when we are in it.

Here's another, which is actually an old hymn:

Work for the night is coming,
Work through the morning hours;
Work while the dew is sparkling;
Work 'mid springing flowers;
Work while the day grows brighter,
Under the glowing sun;
Work, for the night is coming,
When man's work is done.

When I hit my mid forties, I was a fairly successful TV producer. I carried a large packet of antacid tablets in my briefcase, and I went

through a couple dozen of those tablets every day. I also carried a
packet of high-test headache pills, which I took at the first sign of a
headache, which was pretty often. I still carry the headache pills, but
I've managed to get rid of the antacid tablets.

About that time, I wrote an article on "workaholism," and Jim
Taylor, who was editor of *The United Church Observer* at that time, put
in a picture of me
climbing out of my
briefcase. I've got
that picture hanging
in my office because I
still have that monkey
on my back.

Like alcoholism,
you never beat
workaholism. But just
as an alcoholic can
choose not to drink, a
workaholic can
choose not to work
all the time. I can
choose not to let that monkey on my back run my life.

Workaholism is a man's disease. Sure, there are women who have
it. In fact, some feminist women have the worst cases I've ever seen.
But they've caught it from us guys. It's a social disease.

I knew I was a workaholic one day when I was whacking away at a
two-by-four in the shed out back, trying to build some shelves or
something. I didn't have a paying job at the time, and it bugged me.
Suddenly, I wondered where my briefcase was. I dropped my hammer
and ran into the house and found my briefcase. There was nothing in it,
and I didn't need it, but I **had** to know where it was. It was my identity.

We all know guys who have been given the golden handshake, or
the brass handshake, or the tin handshake, or maybe just the old pink
slip. And they still get their identity from the job they used to have. I
was out of a job for a couple of years, and you know what hurt most? I
didn't know who I was. When a couple of guys get into a conversation,
sooner or later they'll start talking about their jobs and that's when my
gut would go into a knot and I'd reach for the antacid tablets.

Men are real men when they have a good job with a fat check, and they work hard, and get a raise, and get more responsibility and bring home a fatter check and get more responsibility and get a raise and they're doing everything right but life is hell. Life is hell, but our friends, our family, the media, the church, all tell us we're doing the right thing.

That's why I recognize the workaholic in King David. He must have worked day and night to keep the whole thing from flying apart. And everybody would tell him what a great king he was, how successful he was, and so he'd keep working because if the kingdom did fly apart, he'd not only lose his job, he'd lose his life.

We work all the time because that's where all the rewards are. And we're haunted by the specter of losing our jobs if we don't work hard. It's not the money, necessarily, though money is a symbol of who we are. If we lose the job, who would we be? Like King David, the job is our life.

So we work even harder, and soon we're out of touch with our family. We start to hide our emptiness with booze or pills. Next thing we know, we're divorced and then we bounce back into another marriage and usually things are not much better because we didn't deal with the original problem.

I'm not totally sure what that original problem is, except it has something to do with the trip we had laid on us about what it means to be a real man. A real man is one who climbs the ladder. Then we get to the top and find it's leaning against the wrong wall.

My father was a workaholic. Except for the nap he took at noon every day, five whole minutes, I don't remember him ever doing anything just for the hell of it. Even when he sat down to read, he always read books that were "worthwhile." He hardly ever played with us kids. My father was very much admired, looked up to in the community.

And I did the same thing. I still do. I work pretty well all the time. When I go on vacation I take my laptop computer so I can work a little along the way. When I'm not doing that, I'm working to keep up the garden or clean out the garage.

So, guys, where and when is the next meeting of the WA. Workaholics Anonymous. I need a meeting. Bad.

Your story

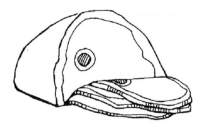

**questions to discuss,
think about,
or write about**

- What kinds of jobs have you had in your life? How important were they to you?
- Have you ever been out of a job? How did that feel?
- Have you ever applied for a job and been turned down?
- If you've never had the experience, imagine what it would be like being a "house-husband." When your male friends ask, "How's it going?" what would you tell them?
- What do you think are the symptoms of workaholism? Was King David a workaholic? Do you know any workaholics? Are you a workaholic?

Chapter 4
Men get turned on

David's story

Part IV
from rapist to lover

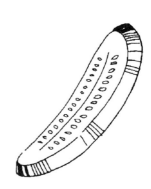

*A loose paraphrase of selected portions
of 2 Samuel.
Chapter 11:1-12:24*

David had everything any man could want.

But there he was, pacing around on the roof of his palace uptight and restless. He tried lying down for a nap. That didn't work. Those unnamed feelings, unfelt fears, unspoken questions seemed to gnaw at his stomach. His prayer life was the pits. He still prayed, but it felt as if he was talking to the wall. He kept thinking of the visit he'd just had from Joab, his second-in-command. David was seething at how damned diplomatic Joab had been, as he tried to get David to stay home from the wars this spring.

Joab hadn't pushed—just hinted that since David had worked so hard, he might need a bit of extra rest. It was true, but David wanted nothing more than to deny it. That old sword he took from Goliath years ago seemed to get heavier and heavier with every fight. "Just can't get the damn thing up anymore," he said, then laughed bitterly at his unintentional double meaning.

David was having a mid-life crisis.

That's when he spotted her. She was there on a nearby roof having a bath. It was her purifying bath following her menstrual period.

Nothing so unusual about that. People often had baths on their rooftops. What was unusual was that David felt his male energies stirring in a way he hadn't felt for a while. None of his wives, none of his concubines made him feel that way any longer. "They're all too old for me," David told himself, knowing it wasn't true. Some of the new concubines were in their teens.

David clapped his hands and a servant came running. "Who is that woman over there on that roof?" he demanded.

"That is Bathsheba. She is the daughter of Eliam and the wife of Uriah the Hittite."

"Go and bring her here."

"But she belongs to…" the servant stammered.

"Never mind who she belongs to," yelled David. "Go get her."

Bathsheba's eyes pleaded "no" when she was brought trembling to David. But David's anger at his impotence inflamed his lust for her. He raped her a few times and sent her home.

David didn't think a whole lot about it. He knew the servant wouldn't squeal and nobody would believe Bathsheba. Then the note came: "I'm pregnant." David knew he was in trouble. There were rules even a king couldn't break.

Uriah, Bathsheba's husband, was off fighting the war with Joab. "Send for Uriah the Hittite," said King David.

"Hey! How's it going?" David was all smiles and handshakes when Uriah came into the palace. "Tell me about the war. Going well, is it?"

"Oh fine, fine," said Uriah, not quite knowing what to make of it all.

"Look, Uriah. You've been working hard. Take a day off. Go home to your good wife. She's gotta be lonely."

"Thank you very much," said Uriah. "That's very kind, sir." But Uriah didn't go home. He slept in the gatehouse, refusing to go to Bathsheba.

"Why didn't you go home and enjoy that beautiful wife of yours, Uriah?" David wanted to know the next morning.

"But sir," said Uriah. "There is a custom in Israel. And even though I am not a Hebrew, I honor it. We do not go down to our homes when our comrades are on the field of battle and sleeping in tents. It's not fair."

"You're a good man," said David, seething inside and worried. "You're a better Hebrew than most Hebrews. So! Let's do lunch. Better yet, let's have dinner tonight. You're the kind of man I'd like to get to know."

It's hard having dinner with the king. When the king says, "Have another glass of wine, Uriah," it's hard to refuse. And the king said that over and over, and Uriah left the palace stinking drunk. But he slept it off in the gatehouse, and didn't go anywhere near Bathsheba.

"Damn!" muttered David. In a fury, he sat down and wrote a note

to General Joab. "Joab: I want Uriah up at the front of the hardest fighting. Then pull back so he's fighting all by himself. I want this man dead. That's an order." David sealed the note, and sent Uriah with his own execution order in his hand, back to the battle front.

When word came back that Uriah was dead, David waited until the appropriate mourning period was over, then brought Bathsheba to the palace. He quickly married her, and sent her off to stay with all his other wives and concubines. In due time, she had a baby boy.

Bathsheba felt confused and violated. Once she even tried to tell King David about her feelings, but he brushed her off. She was just a woman. David had work to do. Case closed.

Except the case refused to stay closed. David found himself visiting Bathsheba more than any of his other wives. Not just for the perfunctory sex that was usual on those visits, but David found himself actually talking with Bathsheba, actually seeking her advice, actually holding and enjoying the baby they had birthed. Not something he ever told his buddies in the army.

Maybe that's why David was hit so hard when Nathan, the prophet, came for a visit. David and Nathan always got along, Nathan often helping David see God's hand in the events around them, sometimes helping David focus on issues of justice in the administration of the nation.

Nathan hadn't been around for awhile, so David was glad to see him. But the prophet looked strained and tired.

"Your majesty," said the prophet. "I've got a situation I'd like to discuss with you."

"Sure," said the king. "Lay it on me."

"Well, it's about these two guys living next to each other. One of them is CEO in his company—five-bedroom mega-house, everything. The other guy rents an old house next door. He's out of a job—on welfare most of the time. He owns a lamb, a pet actually. It's really the only thing he owns. He and his family play with it, they sleep with it. The lamb, in fact, is part of the family.

"One day the rich man next door has some unexpected visitors. He's too cheap to cook his own food, so he sends one of his servants next door to snitch the lamb. And he cooks that for his guests. What do you think should happen?"

"Happen?" David was really angry. "Take that rich guy and string him up by the thumbs! What a rotten thing to do! Can you imagine anyone being so… so…"

"It's you," said Nathan very quietly.

"What?"

"It's you, your majesty. You have a palace full of women and yet you stole Bathsheba from Uriah, then had him killed. Theft. Rape. Murder."

Anger, then shame, then guilt, then remorse flowed across the king's face in succession. Nathan knew the king had the power to kill him for making such an accusation. The silence in the room was long and deafening.

"I have sinned against God," David whispered.

"The punishment for your sin is death," Nathan said quietly, "but God will not take your life. However, the child that was born of your sin will die." Again the silence rang between them. Nathan looked at his friend with anger and compassion. The old prophet loved this complex man who held within him all the best and worst that men can be.

As Nathan had predicted, the child became ill. And David prayed as he had never prayed before, hour after hour, day after day, pleading with God to spare the child, the first child he had ever found the heart to love, born of the only woman he had ever learned to respect. The prayers went on and on; the servants pleaded with David to eat, to sleep, to rest, but David prayed and prayed.

And the child died.

David knew before the servants told him. He saw them whispering among themselves, wondering how to break the news, and whether the king would do something terrible to himself when he heard.

David could feel himself falling apart inside. Struggling to keep control of his emotions, David summoned every bit of strength he had. "C'mon David. Be a man! You've got a job to do," he said to himself. So David put on a brave face, had a shower, put on clean clothes, and ate his first food in a week.

"We don't understand, sir," the servants said. "You fasted and prayed when the child was sick, but now that he has died, you act as if nothing has happened."

David's answer sounded far more brave than he felt. "I hoped to save the child. I hoped God would spare my child. But now he is dead. So no point moping. Let's get on with it."

David began walking to his office, but his legs took him to Bathsheba. "I've got to console Bathsheba," he said to himself as he rejected the thought that he'd never done this when any of the other royal babies had died, as many of them did at birth or soon after. In fact, several wives and concubines had died, but David hardly noticed.

As David entered Bathsheba's room he knew he had not come to console but to be consoled. Together, they shared the gift of tears. They held each other in their pain. And in the months that followed, the bond between them grew. Soon a second child grew within Bathsheba's womb, a child who would bear the name of Solomon.

My story

Sex as we get older

As we get older, we get good at some things.

And I've gotten fairly good at what I do. I'm a wordsmith. I use words to get feelings and ideas across to people, sometimes on the printed page, sometimes in person.

There's a more immediate reward when I do it in person. Sometimes I can almost play an audience the way a conductor plays an orchestra. I can read the faces and I know the time to tell a story or cut the tension with a joke. This is my trade. I work at it. I try to do it well.

There's power in that. When I'm at my best, I feel it is a gift—a sacred trust—and I try to use it openly and responsibly. When I'm at my worst, it becomes a power trip. Most often I am somewhere between those two extremes.

It's taken me years to learn how deal with the comments—the feedback I get from my work. The flattering remarks, especially, are a trap. A deadly trap. When someone says "You're just so wonderful!" there is a part of me that says, "I know."

But here's the toughest time for me. An attractive woman, a few years younger than I am, comes up and, with deep sincerity, says something like, "You really spoke to me. It's as if you knew exactly what was going on inside me. And you shared so much of yourself, I feel I really know you. May I give you a hug?" And then in that hug there is the hint—maybe just in my own mind, but the feelings are strong—the hint that if I held the hug a little longer, pursued the conversation later, something more might happen.

Like every other man who's getting older, I'm bothered by the fact that some things just don't work as well as they used to. I still have the appetite of a 16-year-old, but the rest of me is pushing 60. When my son gives me a hug, I have to tell him, "Mark, be careful. You'll break my ribs." I tell him, laughingly sometimes, that I can do anything he can do, except my recycling time is longer.

That's not true, of course. There are lots of things I can't do at all anymore. Getting older is no fun. My testosterone goes down, which means that some things won't come up. As my sexual powers recede, it's a real temptation to use my other powers to compensate, to avoid the issue of my age. I can write and speak as well as ever. Better probably. But a glance in the mirror after a bath reminds me my speaking ability is about the only thing that's getting better. So when the hugs I get suggest a little more than simple thanks, the yearning to feel young again is there.

> *Therefore a man leaves his father and his mother and clings to his wife, and they become one flesh. And the man and his wife were both naked and they were not ashamed.*
>
> Genesis, 2:24

It's not my strength or will or noble thoughts that save me. I've survived this occupational hazard because I am fortunate. Blessed. Because of Bev, because of family, because of friends, I feel loved. And feeling loved means I don't need to prop up my languishing libido with destructive sex. And I wonder about and ache for other men who don't have such love, who then destroy themselves and others with their power.

It's been said that women give sex to get love and men give love to get sex. I don't know if that's true when we're younger. It certainly becomes less true as we get older. One of God's great gifts, as I grow older with the one I love and trust and cherish, is that the love flows easily back and forth between our bodies without sex. And when sex happens, and it does though not as often, it is but one more soft and beautiful expression of that love.

Our story

Macho is out

OK guys, it's time to change the agenda.
Let's stop talking about women and what they need or what they want or anything else about women. Women are not a big problem. Our society really doesn't suffer a whole lot from womanly traits such as empathy and altruism or nurturing. We can probably handle as much of that as we can get.

The problem is us. Our maleness. We are killing ourselves doing all the things our society wants us to do. At every age, we're dying in accidents, we're shooting each other, we drive cars aggressively, we're two-fisted drinkers, and we have no idea how to handle our sexuality.

As good old Pogo said: "We have found the enemy and he is us."

We keep messing up. It may be as little as telling another sexist joke or as awful as sexual abuse or rape. And then we run to the women in our lives and say, "Please forgive me." And they usually do. Bless them. They shouldn't, but they do.

Or at least they did. Gradually, women are becoming less tolerant. And fellows, while that doesn't feel like good news, it really is.

Not long ago, I had a dream. I was in a church. Not safely behind the pulpit but right out there in the front. With the kids actually. And I was stark naked. Not a stitch. Me in my pot-bellied birthday suit.

I've had that dream before and wondered what it was about. Not this time. The meaning was as obvious as the nose on my face (which, as some of you know, is very obvious).

You see, the night before, I had cranked up the megabytes in my computer and told it to find me stuff for a sermon about the need for change in the context of abuse and forgiveness and reconciliation. "Forgive your enemies." Great sentiment—but if it's going to mean anything, there's got to be a commitment to change.

And my computer let me down. Stupid pile of junk couldn't find what I needed. Annoyed and frustrated, I went to bed.

In my dream I stood in front of the people, with my sermon about forgiveness, and I was stark naked.

I didn't need Joseph or any other guru to interpret my dream. The problem is not with my computer. The problem is with Ralph. I put the data into that hard disk. If there's nothing in my computer about the need for change, it's because there's nothing in my head.

What is in that computer is lots of stuff around forgiving your enemies and what a fine thing that is to do. I could find almost nothing about change as the primary ingredient of forgiveness. I could find no story, no cogent quote that said change and forgiveness are absolutely connected. Without one, the other is cheap and useless.

Before reconciliation and forgiveness, there must be change. It's far too easy for people like David and his modern counterparts just to say "Sorry!" and repeat the same cycle over and over again. Most abusers

---

In Christ we see a truly masculine life lived out with spiritual commitments. In Jesus they were never out of balance. In him we can see the full range of the masculine experience driven by divine life. I believe this fully integrated life is what the Spirit of God is trying to produce in men today. It is not a churchy, phony, unrealistic life. It is an engaging life, filled with human emotion, feeling and tension, yet never without divine perspective, meaning and purpose. It is the kind of life I believe men are looking for in many other places.

Robert Hicks
Uneasy Manhood
Nelson, 1991

are in fact sorry. But not sorry enough to change whatever basic and terrible thing needs changing.

So the time for saying, "I'm sorry" is past. The time has come and now is when we men have to look at ourselves and how we express our sexuality and frankly identify those things that cause pain and havoc in our lives and others. That's going to take more courage, more guts than any war we've ever fought. It's going to hurt more than any injury we've experienced.

If courage and honesty are the hallmarks of real men, we'll do it. We'll stop hiding behind all that macho crap, and come out as the loving, compassionate, caring, free people God intended us to be.

If we really mean it when we say we want world peace, if we really mean it when we say we're against rape and sexual abuse, if we really mean it when we say that we believe all humans are created free and equal, then we'll begin on the only person we can really change. Ourselves.

Your story

questions to discuss, think about, or write about

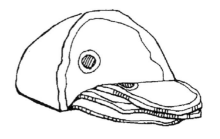

- How has your attitude toward women changed from the time you were a teenager? How is your attitude toward women the same or different than the attitude you see reflected in the beer commercials on TV?
- There's been a lot about sexual abuse and harassment in the media lately. Are things as bad as the media make them out to be?
- Are there things at your place of work, in your community, or in your church that need changing? What could you do about it?
- Have you ever felt uncomfortable when you've heard other men tell sexual jokes that demeaned women? Did you speak out?
- Can you only express disapproval to those you feel are inferior to you—like women and children? Could you ever express disapproval to your boss?

Chapter 5

Men are dads

David's story
Part V
**from workaholic king
to caring father**

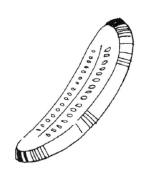

*A loose paraphrase of selected portions of
2 Samuel & 1 Kings:
2 Samuel 12:26-15:31, 18-19:30, 24:1-17
1 Kings 1:1-2:12*

There was little time for wives and babies. David had his work to do.

Joab sent word asking David to come and help fight the Ammonites. "If you don't come and help, I'll take their city and name it after myself," which sounded to David like a bit of power politics. David knew that Joab was not above making a run for David's job, so David did what he had always done so well. He took charge of the operation himself, beat up on the Ammonite cities in the region, took out everything of value, burned them down, killed most of the people, and came home feeling exhilarated. Very masculine. And almost totally exhausted.

Maybe that's why he made such a botch of handling the whole business with his son Amnon and his daughter Tamar.

"Kids," David grumped. "What can you tell them?"

They weren't kids, of course. They were full-grown adults with their gonads goading them into actions that were sometimes despicable. Amnon, David's eldest son, had the hots for his half-sister Tamar. In fact, he made himself sick thinking about her. So he hatched a scheme to get her alone.

Amnon put on an elaborate show of being deathly ill. Naturally King David came to see his son when he heard he was sick. "Anything I can get for you?" he asked.

"Oh yes, father. Could you ask Tamar to come and make me some food. That would be so good."

David should have seen through the silly plot, but he was thinking of wars and politics and found it much easier to avoid contact with his many children. So he told Tamar to go fix some food for Amnon.

Which of course she did. She had no choice. But Amnon pushed the food aside. "I can't eat with all these people around, Tamar," he whined. "Get them out of here so there's just you and me. Then I can relax and eat."

Tamar had no sooner shut the door than Amnon grabbed her. "Come on, sis! Let's do it! I can tell you really want it."

"No! Don't do it, my brother," Tamar pleaded. "Please. Don't! You'll ruin my whole life if you do this. Please..."

But Amnon was stronger than Tamar. Forcing her down on the floor, he raped her.

Tamar lay there, sobbing. Amnon stood up panting. "Get up and get out of here, slut!" he yelled.

"You're just going to use me, then throw me out?" sobbed Tamar. "Don't you realize what you have done to me. Now you're going to throw me out on the street too. What kind of an animal are you?"

"Get this nympho bitch out of here," Amnon yelled to one of the servants. So the servant threw Tamar out and bolted the door after her.

Tamar went to her brother Absalom. She had nowhere else to go. "Well," said Absalom, "he's your brother after all. So don't worry about it, sis. I've got a room in the back of the house you can stay in."

King David of course heard about it, and he was annoyed. But Amnon was his son, his eldest son, and, well, boys will be boys. It's too bad about Tamar, but that's the way things go. Besides, David had more important things on his mind.

Though Absalom had told Tamar to "forget it," he couldn't. He had Tamar there in house, walking around looking like the ruined woman that she was. It took him two full years of stewing about it to get up the nerve, and then he had his servants go and kill Amnon in revenge for what Amnon had done to Tamar.

None of which helped Tamar. Or Absalom who now became a fugitive, on the run from his father who had just lost his crown prince. All of which had David raging around the palace at those "damn crazy kids!"—an anger that was fueled by his suppressed knowledge that he could have prevented the violent destruction of Tamar if he had acted with courage and integrity.

General Joab didn't like what was happening to David and to the politics of the palace. It was important for the welfare of the kingdom to get things back on track, to arrange some kind of reconciliation between David and Absalom. Joab wasn't all that concerned about the issues of justice involved. He just wanted political stability, and family feuds in the palace were not helpful.

Joab went to the town of Tekoa, to get the help of a woman who had a nation-wide reputation for her wisdom. Joab hired her to help solve the problem between David and Absalom.

Maybe the woman had heard how Nathan had handled the rape of Bathsheba. At any rate, she went to David and told him an elaborate story about her two sons, how they fought and one of them got killed, and so the relatives wanted revenge and that would leave her with no sons at all.

David got sucked right into the story. "Two wrongs don't make a right," David pronounced. "Revenge requires more revenge and the whole thing never stops. Tell your relatives to cool it. If they hurt that son of yours, they'll have to answer to me for it."

"Right," said the woman. "Now why don't you live by the same reasoning? Bring your son back into the palace. Two wrongs don't make a right, and a third one even less so."

The king was silent for awhile. "It was Joab who sent you, right?"

"You're the king," said the woman, sitting back. "You know everything."

Another silence. Like Nathan, the woman of Tekoa struggled between her courage and her fear, knowing that at that moment, her life was totally in King David's hands.

"You're right. Of course you're right," said David at last.

But it never really worked out. There were hugs and kisses and tears and apologies. Absalom came back to live in Jerusalem, but the damage had been done. David had never really been a father to his sons, so the reconciliation could not recreate a relationship that had never existed. Everyone could see the tension whenever David and Absalom spoke to each other.

Soon Absalom was plotting to take his father's throne. He became very popular with the crowds. Among other things, he was a hunk with an absolutely glorious head of hair. And Absalom would stand around at the city gate shaking hands, greeting people, and explaining how he

would run the country so much better than his old man.

Four years later, Absalom made his move. On a visit to nearby Hebron, David's home base, Absalom declared himself king. Now the fat was in the fire.

Soon it became obvious that the weight of political power had shifted. Absalom had gained huge power, and David found himself running for his life. Running from his own son. With thousands of people weeping along the side of the road, David and his soldiers left Jerusalem to Absalom.

Absalom may have gained the power, but David still had the smarts of a political street-fighter. He had never forgotten the tricks he'd learned in all his years of struggle to get power and to keep power. By playing hard on people's loyalties and sympathies, by planting spies and "advisors" around Absalom, and by letting everyone know that he was still God's anointed king, David managed to outflank Absalom.

It ended in one big battle in the forest of Ephraim. It was different than the other wars David had fought. "Those were honorable battles," he thought. "This is a family squabble." He knew there would be no winners in this one, only losers.

As the troops marched by, David spoke to his generals. "Take it easy on Absalom, OK?" he said to them. "After all, he is my son."

A forest is not a good place for a battle. The forest claimed more
lives that day than the sword. And the battle quickly turned against
Absalom. Absalom was riding through the forest, when his great head
of hair got caught in an oak tree, and he found himself hanging there,
unable to move. Joab heard about it, rushed over, and killed him. Then
he ordered his men to take Absalom's body and throw it into a pit and
pile stones over it.

That was it. With Absalom dead the battle was over. Nothing
remained but to tell King David. And David reacted as if he was the
loser. Perhaps he was.

"Absalom. Oh my son, Absalom," David wailed. "I wish I had died
instead of you. Oh, Absalom, my son, my son."

Joab and the generals were worried. The king was not getting any
younger. He didn't seem to handle these things as well as he used to.
And Joab was worried about what effect this weeping and wailing for
Absalom would have on the troops.

"Pull yourself together, your majesty," said Joab. "Absalom started
the war, remember? Your men fought hard for you. Some of them died
for you. They saved your life. And here you are weeping for the enemy
you sent us to fight against. Don't your men mean anything to you?"

David struggled for composure. Joab was right, as usual. Focusing
all his inner resources, David swallowed the grief down into his hurting
soul and showed the face that was expected.

For the first time in his life, David felt old. What happened, he
wondered? Life had been so good, and now it seemed to be just one
problem after another. Struggles and intrigues and battles at home, wars
with the Philistines and other neighboring states. Bitterness and anger
seemed to fester through the land. David longed for the day when things
were under control, when things were settled, when people got along.
Should he have ruled with a heavier hand? Had he been too soft on
people? Why did people's anger and hate keep boiling up through the
cracks. Why couldn't people just get along?

David wistfully remembered his vigorous youth when he could
juggle all the balls of state and religion and the military and his family.
But now it seemed so hard to handle even one at any time.

The census was the last straw. It seemed a good idea at the time.
David spent a lot of time in prayer, and he was sure God spoke to him,
told David to assert his authority over people, show them who is boss,
let them know that it is David, King David, who is in charge.

Joab was against it. "People won't like it. It won't do you any good. Doing a census will feel to them like an infringement of the little freedom they have. Every local leader will be mad at you."

"When I want your advice, I'll ask for it!" shouted David. So Joab swallowed hard, set the wheels in motion and got the census done. By Joab's official count, the country had 800,000 men of military age.

But David couldn't help feeling the flak that rolled in from across the country. "Quit your bellyaching!" David yelled out from the roof of his palace one night, at nobody in particular but everyone in general.

It wasn't just the census of course. There was a famine, and a strange and ugly pestilence was creeping through the land. And though he knew he could control neither, David felt the blame and took the burden. David had offered sacrifices and long prayers, asking God for relief from the famine and disease. Things were getting better now, but oh the cost...

Then he remembered Joab's irritating advice. "Joab was right, dammit!" David hissed into the darkness. He pulled his cloak up to his chin against the cold night air. There must be a change in the weather, he thought. It never used to be this cold this time of year. Or maybe he just didn't notice it when he was younger.

The cold in David's bones refused to melt. The servants brought him cloaks and covers, but nothing seemed to help. Then they brought a young girl to the king. Abishag was beautiful. Lithe and lovely, she warmed the king in bed against her nakedness, and though the old man knew that she was his to have, David's body, though not quite his mind, was sexless.

And oh, the old man wished that in his dying he could have the peace of a happy, tranquil family. But peace had not been his throughout his life and was not his now that he was older.

Adonijah, now the eldest son since the death of Absalom, tried to raise an army and to gain support from Joab and the others in a bid to claim the throne. Bathsheba came to David's bedside to plead the case for her son Solomon. "You promised he should be king, not Adonijah," she reminded him.

"Yes, I made a promise to you," David said to Bathsheba. "I promised you that your son Solomon would be king. Well, now's the time. Take Solomon out to Gihon. I want Nathan the prophet and Zadok the priest to anoint him king. Let everyone know that Solomon is now king, and that he will be a greater king than David."

David tried to pronounce the last sentence with strength and conviction, but the words came out rasping and dry. Still, it was done. Solomon became the king, and that struck terror into the heart of Adonijah. He ran into the temple, hoping to find sanctuary there.

His fear gave Solomon the chance to get his reign as king off to a wholesome start: "Tell Adonijah that if he's a good man, things will go well for him. I'm not planning to hurt him." Perhaps the fledgling king glimpsed a vision of a kingship based on justice, not on terror.

David was failing fast. Even beautiful Abishag couldn't keep him warm. Solomon, standing at his father's bedside, reached out his hand. David grasped it hard, and in his dying found a way to be the father he had not been before.

"I'm going to die soon, Solomon," David rasped. "Try to be strong and courageous, and most of all, remember the story. Remember our ancestors and how God was with them through all that happened to them. God has been with me too, in all my life, even though I often didn't pay attention. Faithfulness is the key. Not winning and not being powerful, but being faithful. If you can be faithful with the heritage you have received, God will be with you, my son."

A deep breath, and then another trembled through the frail, royal body. Then it was still.

"My father is asleep with his ancestors," Solomon said to his mother at the door. And she, as any mother would, held the sobbing king, the new king of all of Israel, in her aching arms.

The only revolution that will heal us is one in which men and women come together and place the creation of a rich family life back in the center of the horizon of our values. A letter I got recently from a woman makes the point: "Perhaps the real shift will come when men fully realize, in the gut and not just in the head, that they are equally responsible, with women, for the creation, nurturing, and protection of children—that children are not simple sex objects, ego trips, or nuisances, but their first responsibility—before war, money, power, and status."

by Sam Keen
Fire in the Belly
Bantam Books, 1991

My story

Talking to my dad

I've grieved the death of two good fathers.

My own dad died when I was barely 20. I had left home for school at age 13, and through those teenage years, known him only as the one who gave me lectures when I came home sometimes on weekends. I remember him as strict, authoritarian and a bit of a grouch. I remember him as any rebelling teenager boy remembers his father.

I wish I'd known him as an adult. I wish I'd had the chance to talk with him, man to man, to find out what kind of person he really was. Because mother gave me a scrapbook dad had kept when he was younger. It showed a man of passion, a person of liberality and humor I did not remember.

People who knew him say I remind them so much of my dad. Not just the way I look but the way I act and think and talk. Would he like the rebellious, insolent teenager, now grown to be a man so much like him? Would I like him? Would we be able to talk? Really talk?

The other father was my father-in-law, a fiercely independent man, who left a wealthy family to find his own career. Taciturn and proud, I saw him cry just once —when Bev and I and two small children left for the Philippines. I'm sure he thought we were headed for some god-forsaken jungle and he would never see us again. As the train pulled out of the station, I looked out the window and he was crying.

Even when the emphysema wracked his body, he would not complain. He'd joke a little as he huffed and puffed his way up any slight incline. And as he lay dying on his bed, we played a game that I've relived in my mind so often— wished so much that I could have that time again and could do it right this time.

> Which of you men, if your son asks you for bread, would give him a stone?
>
> Jesus
> Matthew 7:9

Dad knew he was dying. We knew he was dying. He knew we knew. We knew he knew we knew. But why couldn't we talk about it? Why couldn't I say it? "Dad I love you and I really appreciate all you've been to me and to Bev and to our kids. Your life has made a difference to a lot of folks. You've left your mark. The world will be poorer because you're not here. And dad, we're going to miss you terribly."

We didn't say it because then we would have cried. And grown men don't cry, remember? Men keep the stiff upper lip. So I said, "Hey, Dad, you'll be up and around in no time."

And he said, "Take care of those grandkids of mine or you'll have me to answer to when I get out of here."

Why are we like that? Why are we so afraid of what's inside our souls? Why do we hide behind our masks that way, afraid that if we show the self that's real, it won't be good enough? Why do we understand everything except ourselves? Why can we do most everything well, except loving and dying?

So we suppress our secret pain behind our public personality, until the acid eats our hearts, and we go down into our death afraid and so alone.

Our story

The weakest spot

Here are two theories about why we are the way we are.

There's the mustache theory. Men are violent and uptight because they grow mustaches. As support for this theory, all you have to do is look at history. Atilla the Hun had a mustache. So did Joseph Stalin. Adolph Hitler. Saddam Hussein. All of them had mustaches.

All we need is a little electrolysis on the upper lip of every male, and all of society's problems will be solved.

Another theory is that in the good old days when our ancestors wore skins and hunted buck-toothed bison and saber-toothed salamanders for supper, Mr. and Mrs. Og developed different sets of skills.

Osgood Og needs bulging biceps and good hand-eye coordination to throw spears. To miss, or to not throw hard enough, means going hungry—and you can't order chicken from the Colonel. Osgood knows some other hard things. If you stub your big toe on a rock, you can't

call 911. You swallow hard and
keep on hunting, because the
alternative is starving by
yourself in the bush. And if
you're not totally confident that
you can kill that buffalo with
the first spear, and the buffalo
might be a tad annoyed at being
punctured, you swallow your
fear because the alternative is
to hear your belly flapping
against your backbone. Same
holds true if somebody from a
neighboring tribe tries to take
your hunting turf. You fight to
get it back, and if you're
scared, you shove your fear
down inside yourself and fight
anyway.

The folks who hold this theory say that our male genes are pro-
grammed to develop big bones and muscles, good hand-eye coordination and the killer instinct. None of which is particularly helpful when
you spend your days at a sales job. Whacking someone over the head is
not recommended in the books on customer relations. Wringing the
neck of a competitor is considered unfair business practice.

The same theory says that Olga Og learned something else. She
stayed home at camp to look after the kids and the old folks. With all
that family waiting at camp for Dad to bring home supper, she had to
learn how to relate to groups. How to get along.

If that's true, women have the social skills to survive life in the 1990s,
but men, you and I have the social skills of a sophisticated gorilla.

You can call that a load of organic fertilizer. Some of it is. But the
fact is, women, on the average, know more about how to get along with
other folks than men. On the average. Men tend to compete; women
relate. Men know how to father children; women know how to mother.

The only place muscle bulk and good hand-eye coordination is
particularly in demand these days is as a professional athlete. If your
name is Wayne Gretsky or Warren Moon those things are really good to
have, but by the time you're 35 or so, they're as useless as male

mammaries. Anything you can do can be done better, faster and cheaper by a robot. And as for parenting, muscle bulk doesn't really help a bit.

But we've got the old brain. They haven't quite replaced all brains with a computer. Yet. I can be the smartest specialist in any field you name, but if I don't know how to relate to other people, I'll never be able to function in any organization that involves other people. Including a family. And that kind of limits my options.

Here's news. General Bullmoose is dead. Remember him? He was the caricature of the industrial magnate in the Al Capp's cartoon, L'il Abner. He managed his companies the way a bull elephant manages a flower bed.

That way doesn't work any more. Managers are being forced to discover that the people they manage are human beings, with feelings. Big surprise. Push them too much and they tell you exactly into which orifice you may insert your job.

I got technical training in school but no social training. Nowadays they are starting to offer a few life skills but in my day the closest we got to any training in social and sexual relationships was in Phys. Ed. in the summer. Then the girls wore a little less clothing and we got some inkling of what the female body was shaped like. After school, imagination and the older boys filled in some details, but it wasn't too reliable and it didn't deal with women as human beings.

I had a head start on most of the kids. My parents gave me a doll one Christmas, a doll I named Sammy. They encouraged me to play dolls with my sisters. Mom and Dad felt that playing dolls was one way children learned to be parents, and that this was as important for boys as for girls. I kept that a secret from my friends. They would have called me a sissy.

Learning how to be a father I think has something to do with discovering our masculine souls. Learning how to father means learning how to offer strength and nurture to another person, whether that be your own child or another adult.

Until we learn that, until we have found that gentle center to our souls, we have only the macho male to live out, and that will kill us. You and I can keep on doing what Osgood Og did and what a half-back for the Green Bay Packers does. Just keep right on playing through the fear and the pain. My doctor tells me that'll get you in the end. "In your weakest spot, Ralph," he says—which isn't very comforting since my main problem is tension headaches.

It'll get you in your weakest spot too. You may have a heart attack. Or a lower back problem. Or a booze problem. Or an ulcer. Or a divorce. Or suicide. And you may take two or three people, probably people you love, down with you.

Think I'm exaggerating? All those things I mentioned affect men far more than women. To say nothing of higher homicide rates, higher crime rates, earlier death rates.

Osgood Og learned some good things out there in his jungle. But you and I live in a different kind of jungle, where Tarzan and Jane and all their friends and neighbors and co-workers have to learn a different kind of relationship because we all live together in the same little tree house.

Your story

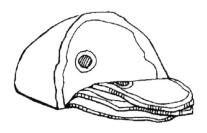

**questions to discuss,
think about,
or write about**

- What is/was your father like?
- What man in your life was the closest thing to a real father that you have experienced? How did he father you?
- How many "fathers" have you had in your life?
- To whom are you a father? From whom did you learn to be a father?
- What does the word "father" mean to you? Is God your father? Does God sometimes relate to you more like a mother?

Another slice of pumpernickel

Men wanna be men

> *The Lord God formed man of the dust of the ground, and breathed into his nostrils the breath of life. And man became a living soul.*
>
> Genesis 2:7

At Naramata Center in the beautiful Okanagan Valley of B.C., Tim Scorer and I found ourselves the only two men in a workshop with about 20 women. Most of them were feminist. Somehow Tim and I ended up leading a worship service based on "male values."

"Are we insane or what?" Tim asked as we began planning for the service. We soon decided that ours was to be a service of celebration. As individuals and as a group men have lots of confessing to do, as do women. But this time we wanted to be able to celebrate manhood, and to celebrate it with our sisters.

We wondered, is that possible?

Tim and I found ourselves working on some very traditional male images. We selected four to reflect on: Father, Warrior, Seeker, Sage.

Father, Warrior, Seeker and Sage are metaphors. A metaphor is a way of speaking—it's a way of describing something that cannot really be described. For instance, if I say, "Look at Gretsky fly!" that's a metaphor. I don't mean that Gretsky literally has wings and can move six inches above the ice. But the metaphor is so much stronger than simply saying, "Gretsky skates fast."

When Bev says to me, "Get out of bed, turkey!" She doesn't literally mean that I am a turkey. It's a metaphor. Or at least, I hope it is.

Metaphors are like snapshots. Each snapshot shows a bit of the truth, even though we know there's always more to the story. I have snapshots of my children looking absolutely angelic, and they were angelic sometimes. Not always. But the snapshots remind me of the statement in the first book of the Bible that we are made in the "image

of God." These snapshots—Father, Warrior, Seeker, Sage—remind me of what men can be at their best. We are not always at our best. There is the bright side of these metaphors, and the shadow side.

Several months after the worship service Tim and I led, I wrote a hymn using those four metaphors. The chorus goes like this:

Father and Warrior, Seeker and Sage,
Gifts of the Spirit for men of our age;
Shared with our sisters and shared with the earth;
Gifts of the Spirit, who brings us to birth.

Father

Masculinity has to do with fathering. That's an interesting word, "fathering." If I "father" a child, it simply means I've gotten a woman pregnant. But if she "mothers" the child, it means she has been nurturing and tender.

But who says men can't be nurturing and tender? When Jesus talked of God as "Father" he wanted us to think of the father in the Prodigal Son story; one who goes out to meet the lost child, who cares and loves deeply. The best of the traditional image of the father incorporates strength, compassion, intelligence and nurturing. That's the model of a father we can work toward and celebrate.

That's the bright side. The shadow side of the Father is the man who rapes, who impregnates and leaves, who dominates and destroys. The shadow side of the Father is the patriarch who sits and rules and has no concern for the weak and the hurting.

The man who simply fathers a baby, then ignores or walks away from the child, is a direct contributor to the violence and abuse we hear about on the news. A number of studies have shown that boys who don't have a nurturing male presence as they grow up are most likely to over-compensate in their need to act like a man. Boys without a father, and boys with violent fathers, are most likely to become violent.

To be a real man means to be a real Father. Not necessarily to beget children of your own, but to be the kind of fathering man who loves and nurtures children and other adults. And a real father wants badly to work in partnership with a mother, because each can offer the child things the other cannot.

Jesus lived the image of a Father when he loved and nurtured children and held them up as good examples of faithful living.

Called to be Father, to sing with a child,
Songs of creation, so restless and wild,
Called to be partner, to nurture, to grow;
Loving to life every seed we may sow.

Warrior

The Warrior metaphor seems a bit harder to deal with. Men already have a tendency toward violence, and so the image of a warrior makes me a little twitchy. It's an image many women find downright frightening, and they have good reasons for their fear. The Warrior image has got more macho crud stuck to it than the other metaphors I'm talking about here. So we have to scrape a little harder.

There is a deep shadow side to the warrior. That's why many people do not like such military metaphors. They have been wounded too often by military men who rape and kill and pillage, by military systems that spend billions of dollars on armaments while people are starving.

But a warrior is far more than just a soldier who obeys orders and who kills others. A warrior has a fire in his belly. A warrior knows exactly what he is fighting for and he is there because he believes in the cause. If we think of the legend of the Knights of the Round Table in King Arthur's court at their very best, we get close to the concept of the Warrior.

The writer of the biblical letter to the Ephesians may have had this kind of Warrior in mind when he asked us to "put on the whole armor of God," to fight against evil, against the "principalities and powers," against the political and social systems that keep some people in poverty and slavery, while others enjoy boundless wealth (Ephesians 6:10-17).

The fundamental question for the Warrior is, "What do I struggle for?" In the best Warrior traditions, the Warrior always fought on the side of the weakest, the poorest, the oppressed. The Warrior fought for justice. It doesn't take much imagination to find issues of justice a man can fight for today.

Some of the Warriors I know are in politics; some at a fairly high level, but most of them live at the grass-roots doing ordinary stuff because they believe in the cause. I know Warriors in the church who "quest for the Holy Grail" of sacred community and truth. Others fight for third-world issues, for peace, or for people here at home. Some are fighting quiet battles at their place of work to defend human dignity or the environment. Some are gently fighting for the life and health of a loved one.

A Warrior is ready to take risks in the struggle. Nowadays, the risks are seldom physical, but they are risks nonetheless. Our jobs, our reputations, our friends may all fall as casualties in our struggle for justice.

Yes, of course, many of the people who struggle for justice are women. But men in the warrior tradition have a slightly different style than women. Sometimes men and women work together, pooling their complimentary skills, and then good things can happen.

Jesus was a Warrior who argued and fought and put his life on the line in his struggle for people on the margins of society, in his passion for Shalom, for true peace and justice.

Called to be Warrior, in quest of the Grail,
Striving for justice, to triumph or fail,

Strong with our sisters, we answer the call
Bravely and gently to be patient with all.

Seeker

Men have a strong tradition of the Seeker or the Quester. The Seeker is willing to "boldly go where no man has gone before." That's why so many men enjoy the Star Trek series. It appeals to the Seeker within them.

Seekers have always wondered what lies beyond the next horizon. It takes courage to leave the known and the secure, to break new ground, to chart new territories.

Sometimes that's exploring countries and continents or the surface of the moon. But now more often, the Seeker is the one who dares to think new thoughts, to explore new ideas. Most of all, the Seeker is willing to go within himself, to learn of both the dark side of his violent inner nature, and the bright side—the man willing to risk true understanding. It's the Seeker in you that has kept you reading this book and wondering about the questions it poses.

The shadow side of the Seeker is the Peter Pan, the eternal boy who cannot commit himself to anyone or anything, who flits from one idea to another, from one relationship to another. Peter Pan can be a charming person but he lacks one essential quality: commitment.

In his quests, the Seeker is often joined by women who, like the Seeker, are looking for better ways to be more creatively human together.

Jesus was a Seeker who was willing to follow truth into the desert and into death and beyond.

Called to be Seeker, to search deep within
For anger and violence that leads us to sin,
Travel new paths never journeyed before;
Learn with our sisters, what God has in store.

Sage

The Sage is not a guru who dispenses knowledge, but rather a man who is able to think below the surface of things, to put words around ideas, around truth, no matter how inadequate. The Sage doesn't put much faith in easy answers or slogans.

Most importantly, the Sage is able to ask the question, and to live with the knowledge that there is often no answer. In fact, the Sage knows that sometimes the answer is not nearly as important as the question.

The shadow side of the Sage is the "know-it-all" who claims to understand everybody else's problems and to have complete and workable cures for everything. The shadow side of the Sage is the man who has taken up the full-time vocation of complaining about the government, about "young people nowadays" and to dispensing instant solutions to the world's problems. That kind of "pseudo-Sage" has lots of answers, but doesn't know what the questions are. He does a lot of talking, but very little listening.

The Sage is able to hear the wisdom spoken by children, to hear the truth in the simple words of those who have little formal education. And the irony is that, while the Sage has a deep sense of how little he knows, he is full wisdom and insight.

The Sage, with his female counterpart, the wise old woman, sits on the front porch ready to offer help and comfort and a listening ear to anyone who asks.

Jesus was a Sage who loved simple people, and who told parables.

Called to be Sage, to reflect and to know
Words around truth so our spirits may grow;
Dancing the gifts we've suppressed and denied—
Sing with our sisters, as we grow side by side.

Other metaphors

There are, of course, many other images of masculinity. If those above don't suit you, develop your own. We need metaphors to talk about these kinds of realities. The language of science simply doesn't apply in this area.

Heeding the collective lament of women in recent decades, many men have reconsidered time-honored tenets of manhood. They have become gentler and more open. They have reconstructed their behavior.

Yet somehow, anticipated healing between the sexes has not come. In the softening process, men appear to have lost whatever strength they had, and some are wondering if, on the whole, men of recent generations ever had the right kind of strength.

Prodded by archfeminists, caricatured and condescended to by TV scriptwriters, and unsure about how to work for or with women on the job and in the home, they are coping with outward pressures and interior forces they don't always comprehend. They feel confused, misunderstood, hurt, and angry. Past heroes are gone, and a splintered society provides few unifying models of manhood.

Larry Haise
Bookstore Journal
January, 1992

None of us have arrived. All of us are wondering how we can be authentically male in an era when traditional male values seem, on the surface at least, to be crumbling, when men are the butt of most sit-com jokes on TV, when marriages and families are breaking up and men feel themselves blamed.

We can get together and talk about it, and metaphors such as the ones I've used in this chapter can help sometimes. I've found such talking has helped me, even though at first I wondered if the guys would simply laugh at my confusion.

I've been to a number of men's weekends in various parts of the country. Each time I've gone with a sense of unease wondering what I was letting myself in for. Then I found the men at the weekend were pretty much in the same boat. On the surface, everything was fairly normal, but deep down we were running scared.

I'd heard some standup comics make fun of "men's libbers" who ran naked through the bush, who beat on drums and chanted, who learned how to cry together... I'm past middle age and pretty conservative about lots of things, and the media didn't make it sound as if I'd feel very comfortable in those kinds of groups. When I asked a few questions, I found out that those kinds of groups are the exception rather than the rule.

The men's groups I've been part of didn't do anything spectacular. We did a lot of talking, about darn near everything. We played a little golf and drank a lot of coffee and talked with each other. It seemed like a safe place to get my head sorted out around problems I'd never been able to put words to before. Nobody came up with any brilliant solutions, but talking about it helped me clarify my own thinking about myself. Now I think I know what I want to be when I grow up. Since I'm pushing 60, it's probably time I did.

Jesus once said that wherever two or three are gathered, he's there with them. Even though the talk didn't sound very religious in those men's groups, I really felt the presence of Jesus there with us. He seemed to be saying, "Yeah, I know what it's like to be a man. It's not always a picnic, I know that."

The exciting thing I learned from these groups is that being a man can be fun. It's a grand, creative time to be a man. We can celebrate and enjoy who we are and the way God has created us. We can let go of the things that hurt us and destroy ourselves and others. We can kick up our heels and genuinely enjoy the gifts of the other people in our lives: our wives, our partners, our children, or colleagues, our friends. Unlike my dad who didn't even know he had a tape playing in his head, I can turn off the tape in my head.

No, I don't want to turn it off, because there are parts of it that are really good. Now I can **select** what I'm going to pay attention to. I'm becoming my own man.

Getting rid of some of the male hangups reminds me of the clergyperson who told me why he wore a stiff clerical collar. "Because it feels so good when you take it off."

All of which brings us back to those "dumb male" jokes.

What's the difference between government bonds and men?
Government bonds will eventually mature and be worth something.

Have a good laugh at that, then look at it again. Then throw this book in the corner and say, "Go to hell, Milton! I am mature, and I am worth something!" Because it says right there in the first chapter of the Bible that you and I and our sisters are all made "in the image and likeness of God." And as the old Sage said, "God don't make no trash."

Liberation is throwing aside all the crap in our heads that keeps us from being the real men God intends us to be: real men, who are Fathers, Warriors, Seekers and Sages and who, side by side with our sisters, can work with God to create the peace and justice, the Shalom God intended for all of humanity.

It's like taking off a tight pair of shoes. It's like opening a door in a stuffy room. I am amazed at the freedom that comes with being a 'liberated man" even though that sense of liberation feels pretty thin when I discover yet another skeleton in my emotional closet. But each time I do open those doors, I let in a bit more air and let out a bit more stuffiness. Slowly, beautiful things are beginning to grow again in my soul.

I enjoy being a man.

And man, that feels good!

Notes:

The service of worship referred to at the beginning of this chapter is included in the *Man to Man Study Kit*. Congregations which have purchased that kit, or which subscribe to *LicenSing*, may reproduce the words to the hymn *To Be A Man* for use in the congregation. Others may contact Wood Lake Books (address below). The hymn can be sung to the tune Slane (usually sung for the words, "Be Thou My Vision").

While you can, of course, read this book by itself, it is intended to be part of that kit. In the kit are materials for five sessions where a group of men (not less than four) can play some games, have a few laughs, listen to some bits of tape, and generally have a good time. You'll find it easy to talk about the issues raised in this book, and you'll develop some good friendships in the process.

The kit is available through many bookstores, and directly from:

Wood Lake Books
Box 700
Winfield, British Columbia
Canada V0H 2C0
order line 1-800-663-2775

Logos Productions Inc.
P. O. Box 240
South St. Paul, MN 55075
USA
1–800–328–0200

MediaCom
PO Box 610 Unley
South Australia
5061
toll free tel. 008–811–311

Other books by Ralph Milton

Living God's Way; Bible stories for children in today's world
Hardcover • $ 26.95 • *Softcover* • $ 16.95

This United Church of Ours • $ 12.95

The Gift of Story • $ 9.95

Common sense Christianity • $ 11.95

Through Rose-Colored Bifocals • $ 9.95

Also available from Wood Lake Books

The I Can Attitude
By Dennis Oliver

Approach your health, relationships, job, and faith in a positive and constructive way.
929-083 • **$ 12.95**

The Quietness Book
By Ray Ashford
Inspiring quotes, excerpts and sayings which encourage reflection and meditation.
929-087 • **$ 12.95**

Available from: Wood Lake Books, PO Box 700, Winfield, BC V0H 2C0

1-800-663-2775